More How to Win
at Aptitude Tests

More How to Win at Aptitude Tests

Liam Healy

Thorsons

Thorsons
An Imprint of HarperCollins*Publishers*
77-85 Fulham Palace Road
Hammersmith, London W6 8JB

The Thorsons website address is:
www.thorsons.com

First published 2001

10 9 8 7 6 5 4 3 2 1

© Liam Healy

Liam Healy asserts the moral right to be
identified as the author of this work

A catalogue record of this book is available
from the British Library

ISBN 0 00 711257 2

Printed and bound in Great Britain by
Omnia Books Limited, Glasgow

All rights reserved. No part of this publication may be
reproduced, stored in a retrieval system, or transmitted,
in any form or by any means, electronic, mechanical,
photocopying, recording or otherwise, without the prior
written permission of the publishers.

Contents

Introduction

Welcome and well done. You have probably picked up this book for one of three reasons:

1 You, or someone you know, are about to take some aptitude tests and you think you may need a hand;
2 You are facing some choices regarding your own career and you want to find out what you are good at and what you are not so good at;
3 You have heard about aptitude tests and know that a lot of companies use them for recruitment or development purposes, so you want to brush up your skills – just in case.

The numerous test examples and detailed information in this book will help you prepare for test sessions, and give you an idea of what to expect during an actual test session, so reducing your anxiety about having to face what can be the most daunting part of a recruitment process. The reasons why companies use tests to make decisions and how they use them, are explained. Tests are very often followed by post-test feedback and interviews, and the best approaches to these are described.

Practice Tests

In this book you will find examples of the most common

types of test in use today, as well as examples of some of the less common. For every type of test, preparation and practice strategies are included, as well as detailed answers to the questions. For the most basic ability tests, through to graduate and managerial level reasoning and problem-solving tests, this book is likely to be your best single source for preparing for that all-important test.

With the increasing emphasis companies place on the 'softer' behavioural skills, a specially written personality test has also been included – you are more likely to face this type of test than any other. This will help give you a complete picture of what you are like as a person. Whatever type of test you are going to face, this book will show you what to expect.

Reduce Your Anxiety About Being Tested

It is only natural that when faced with an unknown task you will be nervous. This is true whether you are a school leaver applying for your first job, or a senior executive applying for your final post before retirement. Aptitude testing is used for more than just recruitment; for many companies it plays a pivotal role in development as well – in either case, knowing what to expect will enable you to produce a performance which is less hindered by nerves and which reflects more closely your actual skills and abilities.

Handling the Selection Process

Being invited to sit a test (or tests) is only one part of the selection process. This book explains what tools an employer may use to assess the skills and abilities that they are interested in. The other types of selection tool you may also come across, such as assessment centres, interviews, work samples and job simulations, are also described.

Because most employers use structured interviews to validate the results of tests, the post-test interview is covered in detail. This includes advice on how to recover if you think your performance has been less than perfect!

Whatever you choose to do in your life – and it is your life and happiness which are important, not simply your career – this book gives you the chance to prepare yourself for some of the challenges you may face.

Good luck!

1

About Aptitude Tests

An aptitude test is one of a larger group of measures of psychological characteristics collectively known as 'psychometric tests'. Overall, psychometric tests fall into one of two categories:

1 **Tests of Typical Performance** – which include things such as personality tests and interest questionnaires.
2 **Tests of Maximum Performance** – which include things such as aptitude and ability tests.

TYPICAL AND MAXIMUM PERFORMANCE

Typical Performance Test

A typical performance test looks at what you can typically do. This means measuring what you can do without any real effort or preparation.

Personality questionnaires

The most common type of typical performance test is the personality questionnaire, but they can also be used to measure things such as work preferences and interests. Personality questionnaires usually contain items (or questions) in the form of:

Q I would rather go out and socialize with my friends than stay in and read a book.

A (choose one)   Agree ☐   Disagree ☐

Clearly, there is no 'correct' answer to this question. Assuming that a question measures a personal trait such as 'enjoyment of social contact', there is no particular meaning or value attached to either answer. In other words, neither answer is intrinsically good or bad. So, for instance, saying that a person scored 23 out of 56 on an assertiveness scale is probably meaningless, while saying that they were more assertive than average might have some relevance to their suitability for employment. Most typical performance tests, such as personality questionnaires, have no time limit, although, for organizational efficiency, some test supervisors may encourage you to complete them within a set time.

Tests of interest and tests of motivation

There are two other types of typical performance test you may come across – tests of interest and tests of motivation. Tests of interest are rarely used in selection processes, being more commonly used in career development. Tests of motivation are just that – measures of what motivates a person. However, they are quite rare and very seldom used in selection, not least because no one can agree what exactly tests of motivation should be looking for.

Maximum Performance Tests

A maximum performance test looks at what you can actually do when you are trying your best and this is exactly what an aptitude or ability test is. Look at the following from a numerical aptitude test:

123 x 456 = ?

Clearly, if you do not put effort into answering this question, you will not get the answer right. Your gut feeling might produce an answer of about 500,000. This is not the correct answer, and if you put this down as the answer you would be wrong. If you tried harder you might eventually come up with the correct answer (56,088).

So, with tests of maximum performance, the questions *do* have right and wrong answers and so the results can be interpreted numerically with greater ease than typical performance tests.

One of the things we know about intellectual ability is that people who are rated as being more intelligent than others may be so because they can solve problems more quickly. It follows that tests of maximum performance, such as aptitude tests, usually have strict time limits.

ABILITY AND APTITUDE

If you sat a test that assessed your numerical skills, you may find that it would be called something like a 'Numerical Aptitude' test. Subsequently, you may sit a test that looks exactly the same but instead is called a 'Numerical Ability' test. They certainly look the same – but there is a difference.

In reality, they both measure numerical skills. Psychologists have known for a long time that intelligence, or intellectual ability, is composed of a number of separate facets. Generally, these areas are accepted as being linked to verbal, numerical, abstract, spatial and mechanical reasoning.

If we were only interested in, say, mechanical reasoning, we would refer to this very specific area as 'aptitude' or 'specific ability'. Very often, a person's scores on three tests – for example, verbal, numerical and abstract ability – are combined to produce an overall score. More rarely, because of the time involved, a test may have questions from all three.

When used in this combined way, a measure of a person's overall general ability or general aptitude is obtained. Remember:

Ability = general aptitude or overall ability at verbal, numerical and abstract thinking.

Aptitude = specific ability, such as in verbal or numerical or abstract thinking.

This distinction is not so important for the average test taker, since you may simply be told to expect a test of numerical reasoning skill, so don't worry too much about it.

It is important, though, not to confuse tests of ability and aptitude with tests of attainment. These assess what you have learnt, and are tests of knowledge not ability. Things like school or driving exams are tests of attainment rather than direct measures of ability.

SPEED AND POWER TESTS

Speed and Power tests represent different *styles* of test, rather than measuring different aptitudes or abilities; specifically, they describe the nature of the test questions themselves.

In a speed test, the items tend to be quite small in scope, very specific and often not too difficult. With speed tests it is *how many* questions the test taker can answer correctly that is important. A numerical aptitude test with speed items could look something like this; you can see how each question is very narrowly confined in terms of content:

$123 + 456 = ?$
$987 - 654 = ?$
$567 \times 123 = ?$

In the case of a power test, the approach is quite different and much more emphasis is placed on presenting the test taker with a smaller number of more difficult or complex questions.

A numerical aptitude test with power items may look something like:

Brian is 6 cm taller than Kate and Kate is 2 cm taller than William. William is 1,680 cm tall. Andrew is taller than all three but not as tall as Marjorie.

Brian is taller than Andrew   a) true b) false c) can't tell
Brian is 1,692 cm tall   a) true b) false c) can't tell

Typically, speed tests contain a lot more items than power tests although they often have the same approximate time limit. Power tests tend to be used more at the graduate, professional or managerial level since their expanded format allows for more work-related content to be addressed.

APTITUDE AND REASONING ABILITY

Although reasoning ability does depend on some level of 'raw' or basic ability, aptitude and reasoning ability are two different things. Straightforward ability or aptitude is to do with the computational acts involved in solving a very specific test question – what you have to do is often clear, whether you can do it or not is quite a different matter. Reasoning ability is to do with knowing *when* to apply a certain computational act.

In the power and speed test examples above, the speed questions were to do with basic, raw numerical or mathematical ability. A very precise act of computation (for instance subtraction or multiplication) was clearly indicated by the format of the question. All you had to do was carry out the calculation.

With the power questions, it was not indicated which specific mathematical computation (for instance, addition or division) had to be carried out in order to reach a solution. The task you faced was to apply a more general problem solving approach – the problem being not 'what is the answer?' but 'what do I have to do to work out how to reach the answer?'

Once you have established how to reach the answer, the final task itself is often a very simple process of mathematical calculation.

Brian is 1,692 cm tall   a) true   b) false   c) can't tell

If William is 1,680 cm tall, Kate is 2 cm taller than William, and Brian is 6 cm taller than Kate then the answer must be:

1,680 cm + 2 cm + 6 cm = 1,688 cm.

So the statement that Brian is 1692 cm tall is false.

Notice how simple the mathematics was once we had worked out what to do. This is a good example of numerical

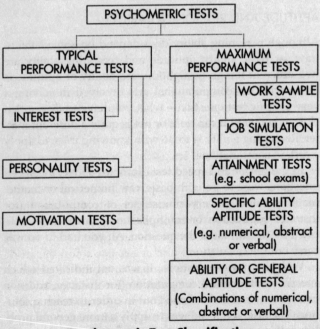

Psychometric Test Classification

reasoning ability or aptitude, rather than just straight-forward numerical ability or aptitude. Furthermore, because the information is presented verbally, this is also a reasonable example of what verbal reasoning test items may look like. Power tests are more commonly found in the numerical and verbal domains but can also crop up in the mechanical, abstract and perceptual ability areas.

OTHER TYPES OF TEST

The other two commonest types of test are Work Samples and Job Simulations, although at first glance they do not look as we imagine tests to be.

A Work Sample test is exactly what its name implies – a sample of the work the candidate is required to do. These tend to be used widely in mechanical or practical areas of work. A common example is a typing test where the candidate has to type out some hand-written notes without making any errors within a given period of time. Another example is a fork-lift truck driver moving a set number of pallets from one place to another to within a certain degree of accuracy. If you are invited for a Work Sample test, the chances are you already have some skill in the area to begin with.

Job Simulations look similar to Work Samples and the two are often confused. However, whereas a Work Sample actually involves doing a sample of the activities carried out in the target job, a Job Simulation only simulates those activities involved in the target job.

If our fork-lift truck driver was inexperienced, it would clearly not be wise to put him or her into a fork-lift truck and see how little damage is done! It would be better to measure those abilities we know are involved in driving a fork-lift truck, such as hand to eye co-ordination, spatial awareness and so on, and then use the information obtained to infer how the person might perform in the job once they had been trained. Because of this, Job Simulations are often used when selecting people for training or when they have no direct experience in or specific knowledge of the job in question.

Another common type of Job Simulation is the so-called 'In-basket', or 'In-tray', which is used for many management-based selection activities. The In-tray simply involves taking the contents of a manager's typical in-tray and working through them, making decisions as to what to do with each item as you go. These simulations are often used to assess organizational and decision-making ability, and are quite commonly used in management selection. However, you do need the contents of a real in-tray to base the exercise on and these contents can be both numerous and diverse – an entire in-basket could easily fill this book!

In addition, tests like In-trays are very difficult to score correctly because there is often no single correct way to deal with the items. Consequently, they tend to be followed up by a presentation from, or interview with, the candidate during which they explain how they worked their way through the in-tray, what criteria they used for decision making and how they justified their actions.

HOW AND WHY COMPANIES USE APTITUDE TESTS

Where Do Tests Fit into the Wider Selection Process?

The purpose of a selection system is to make a prediction about who will be successful at the job. It does this by gathering evidence about a candidate, weighing that evidence and then making a decision as to whether or not to offer them a position.

One thing that many candidates mistakenly believe is that the test constitutes the complete selection process. In fact, tests are very rarely used as a first stage in selection. Usually, the process begins long before a job is advertised and typically it involves the following steps.

Job Analysis

This is carried out to determine the key tasks of the job. It can involve sophisticated analytical methods using data about several hundred job holders, or it can be done using 'expert analysis' which involves a group of individuals, who are very familiar with the job, sitting down and agreeing what the job involves. In cases where there are relatively few employees (which rules out large-scale statistical analysis) the latter method tends to be used.

Producing the Job Description

This is a formal description of the tasks identified as a result of the job analysis.

Producing the Person Specification

This often takes quite a lot of work. The key challenge for the organization here is to identify the knowledge, skills, attributes and abilities a person must possess if they are to be able to carry out the tasks described in the Job Description. Very often these characteristics, contained in the Person Specification, are classified as being either 'essential' or 'desirable'.

Identifying What the Success Criteria Will Be

This involves setting success criteria for future work performance for use in work appraisals. This stage is often overlooked, but it remains an important part of the process since it allows the organization to analyze how well their selection system and selection tools actually predicted work success.

Choosing the Selection Tools

The selection tools are then chosen based on their effectiveness at measuring those characteristics described in the Person Specification. They may include interviews, tests, CVs, application forms, and individual or group exercises.

Applying the Chosen Selection Tools

This is often done in several stages, with successful candidates at one stage being invited to participate in the next. Sometimes, candidates may be pre-selected based on qualifications or experience, and then invited to come along to an assessment day (sometimes known as an assessment centre), during which all of the tools are used.

Weighing Evidence Gathered From the Selection Tools

Usually, no single assessor has the final say over any one candidate. In the case of assessment centres in particular, an observation and scoring system is devised which means that different assessors observe different candidates over the course of the day, and the ratings allocated to each candidate by each assessor are scored using a standardized scoring system. Conflicting evidence is discussed and an overall rating is agreed upon by the whole assessment team. This occurs after the assessments have been carried out and the candidates have gone home.

Making a Selection Decision

This is based on the evidence that has emerged from the assessment process. The decision as to whether or not to offer someone a job is seldom solely based upon the need to hire someone, rather it is based upon the evidence. It is not uncommon for an organization not to hire any of the candidates they have seen, especially if all of the candidates have weaknesses in one or more 'essential' areas of the person specification.

The final decision can be based on a simple test score 'cut-off' as a first stage (where test scores are clearly related to job performance). A more sophisticated process might involve 'regression' or 'factor analysis', and a 'multi-stage actuarial decision process'. But these are in the realms of advanced selection theory and beyond the scope of this book.

There is no use in worrying about it – you can't influence the decision making process, mainly because you will not be there when it goes on! Do bear in mind that if this process has been gone through thoroughly by the organization, you can take some comfort from the fact that the selection or recruitment process and decision-making mechanism are based on evidence and have been designed to be as objective and error free as possible. The fact that an organization uses tests should be viewed as a source of comfort rather than dread.

WILL I ONLY COME ACROSS TESTS WHEN I APPLY FOR A JOB?

The answer to this question is probably 'No'. When one considers the type of information a test produces, it is clear that the information can be broadly classified into two areas:

1 This person has the ability that is required.
2 This person does not have the ability that is required.

When looked at like this, the outcome from a test can also be used very effectively in development. This is particularly the case with the 'softer' behavioural skills which personality tests assess.

Tests are also used extensively in Career Development work, often in conjunction with a Personal or Career Development Plan.

FINALLY, THE TESTS!

In the following chapters we will go through example tests. For some types of test there is quite a bit of background involved. This is because areas such as numerical ability can cover a wide range of information and are applicable to many different types of job. Numerical ability testing is one area people worry about more than any other, so there is more space given to this. Other areas, such as mechanical reasoning, are more straightforward, more self-explanatory. The main categories of aptitude tests covered are:

Basic Numerical Ability – These tests measure basic mathematical ability.

Numerical Reasoning – These tests measure higher-level or more complex problem solving where the problems are numerical in nature.

Basic Verbal Ability – These tests measure basic verbal abilities such as spelling and comprehension.

Verbal Reasoning – These tests measure higher-level or more complex problem solving where the problems are verbal in nature. They are sometimes known as 'critical thinking' tests.

Abstract Reasoning – These tests measure problem solving ability in a context-free environment and are largely based on non-verbal and non-numerical questions.

Spatial Reasoning – These tests measure the ability to perform operations such as rotation or combining different features of two- and three-dimensional objects in one's head.

Mechanical Reasoning – These tests measure the ability to work out how different mechanical operations and physical principles affect objects.

Perceptual Ability – These tests measure the ability to take in and manipulate verbal, numerical and other textual information.

For each test you will also see a classification system which will tell you how that particular test is used, how long it is likely to be, and other relevant information, such as the level of difficulty. The format used is as follows:

Test 1 Name

Type of test: Speed, power or both.

Typical length: The typical number of questions in the test.

Typical time allowed: How long one is typically allowed to complete such a test.

Used for: The type of job it tends to be used for. These are classified as:

Basic, such as clerical, or jobs with occasional requirements for this ability, but mostly at a simple or basic level.

Intermediate, such as supervisory or junior management jobs which require more frequent or complex use of this ability.

Higher, such as professional, middle and senior management, or specialist types of work which require frequent use of this ability in high-level problem solving situations.

Frequency of use: Whether the test is in common use or is used less often. We have focussed on those types of tests that are in common use.

Remember that this information is only a guide. The actual tests you may face are likely to vary in how closely they match those given in this book.

At the end of each test, or each set of similar tests, you will find hints and tips that provide suggestions for how to prepare for and approach that particular type of test.

In Chapter 8, there is more detailed information on exactly what to do to prepare yourself for the testing session and what happens afterwards.

The answers to all of the tests, plus an explanation where appropriate, are in Appendix I at the end of this book.

Finally, in Chapter 7 we go through an example of a Personality Test. Full scoring instructions are given with the test, but remember – with personality tests there are no right or wrong answers. Only you will know what is right!

2
Numerical Tests

Numerical ability tests fall into one of two camps – outright mathematical ability requiring you to carry out mathematical calculations, and numerical problem-solving ability requiring you to work out what mathematical calculations you should apply, rather than just telling you. This second type is referred to as numerical reasoning and tends to have more of a power than speed design.

In the case of mathematical ability, the type of calculation you are expected to perform will usually be made clear to you. Our first set of five tests looks at mathematical ability.

Note that the numbers involved are not too complex – it would be beyond most people to calculate $2654 \div 13$ in their head! Also, note that you are not given a set of answers from which to choose. The rationale behind this is that if you can work out the correct answer then you can simply write it down, and if you can't work out the answer then guessing won't help much.

Tests 1–5 concentrate on basic mathematical computation or calculation. Try them, they will act as a useful warm up for the numerical tests later on which are to do with applying mathematical ability to real world problems.

Numerical Test 1 (Addition)

> **Type of test:** Speed
>
> **Typical length:** 25–35 questions
>
> **Typical time allowed:** 20–30 minutes
>
> **Used for:** Basic level
>
> **Frequency of use:** Common

In this test your task is simply to calculate the correct answer. Give yourself 20 minutes.

1   $7 + 45 =$
2   $15 + 21 =$
3   $9 + 57 =$
4   $215 + 37 =$
5   $12 + 6 =$
6   $154 + 45 =$
7   $39 + 22 =$
8   $17 + 89 =$
9   $25 + 98 =$
10   $21 + 75 =$
11   $54 + 4 =$
12   $14 + 25 =$
13   $102 + 14 =$
14   $19 + 16 =$
15   $17 + 7 =$
16   $22 + 9 =$
17   $5 + 18 =$
18   $8 + 14 =$
19   $3 + 19 =$
20   $45 + 5 =$
21   $165 + 14 =$
22   $48 + 5 =$
23   $112 + 54 =$
24   $97 + 81 =$

25	25 + 52 =
26	44 + 57 =
27	8 + 46 =
28	13 + 67 =
29	19 + 28 =
30	20 + 15 =

Numerical Test 2 (Subtraction)

> **Type of test:** Speed
>
> **Typical length:** 25–35 questions
>
> **Typical time allowed:** 20–30 minutes
>
> **Used for:** Basic level
>
> **Frequency of use:** Common

In this test your task is simply to calculate the correct answer. Give yourself 20 minutes.

1	12 – 107 =
2	54 – 58 =
3	8 – 96 =
4	23 – 101 =
5	65 – 135 =
6	79 – 65 =
7	24 – 47 =
8	29 – 21 =
9	13 – 29 =
10	168 – 64 =
11	9 – 35 =
12	185 – 18 =
13	36 – 57 =
14	48 – 67 =
15	57 – 24 =
16	59 – 32 =

17 $24 - 152 =$
18 $65 - 144 =$
19 $72 - 33 =$
20 $12 - 225 =$
21 $9 - 49 =$
22 $208 - 26 =$
23 $26 - 53 =$
24 $7 - 118 =$
25 $38 - 52 =$
26 $61 - 34 =$
27 $109 - 81 =$
28 $42 - 22 =$
29 $48 - 18 =$
30 $153 - 62 =$

Numerical Test 3 (Division)

Type of test: Speed

Typical length: 25–35 questions

Typical time allowed: 20–30 minutes

Used for: Basic level

Frequency of use: Common

In this test your task is simply to calculate the correct answer. Give yourself 30 minutes.

1 $21 \div 7 =$
2 $15 \div 3 =$
3 $66 \div 11 =$
4 $111 \div 37 =$
5 $45 \div 9 =$
6 $64 \div 16 =$
7 $39 \div 13 =$
8 $36 \div 12 =$

9	$25 \div 25 =$
10	$190 \div 19 =$
11	$80 \div 4 =$
12	$75 \div 25 =$
13	$78 \div 13 =$
14	$110 \div 10 =$
15	$122 \div 2 =$
16	$95 \div 5 =$
17	$70 \div 7 =$
18	$54 \div 27 =$
19	$16 \div 4 =$
20	$63 \div 7 =$
21	$170 \div 10 =$
22	$10 \div 1 =$
23	$74 \div 2 =$
24	$60 \div 3 =$
25	$125 \div 25 =$
26	$250 \div 5 =$
27	$300 \div 60 =$
28	$390 \div 13 =$
29	$99 \div 9 =$
30	$160 \div 20 =$

Numerical Test 4 (Multiplication)

Type of test: Speed

Typical length: 25–35 questions

Typical time allowed: 20–30 minutes

Used for: Basic level

Frequency of use: Common

In this test your task is simply to calculate the correct answer. Give yourself 25 minutes.

1   12 x 6 =
2   17 x 5 =
3   5 x 16 =
4   69 x 3 =
5   17 x 7 =
6   6 x 15 =
7   2 x 127 =
8   8 x 9 =
9   15 x 15 =
10 65 x 4 =
11 9 x 32 =
12 32 x 10 =
13 44 x 3 =
14 17 x 54 =
15 13 x 5 =
16 6 x 120 =
17 19 x 8 =
18 4 x 45 =
19 6 x 50 =
20 7 x 35 =
21 12 x 9 =
22 21 x 4 =
23 9 x 13 =
24 25 x 10 =
25 4 x 37 =
26 13 x 7 =
27 28 x 5 =
28 45 x 9 =
29 120 x 5 =
30 55 x 5 =

Numerical Test 5 (Combination)

> **Type of test:** Speed / Power
>
> **Typical length:** 25–35 questions
>
> **Typical time allowed:** 20–35 minutes
>
> **Used for:** Basic level
>
> **Frequency of use:** Common

In this test your task is simply to calculate the correct answer. Give yourself 35 minutes.

1   $5 \times 6 + 11 =$
2   $6 + 12 - 8 =$
3   $1 \times 5 \div 5 =$
4   $25 \times 10 \div 25 =$
5   $4 + 7 \times 4 =$
6   $23 \times 10 - 150 =$
7   $22 + 20 \times 3 =$
8   $9 \times 30 \div 27 =$
9   $8 \times 45 + 10 =$
10 $16 \times 25 \times 2 =$
11 $66 - 8 \times 5 =$
12 $15 - 5 \div 2 =$
13 $4 \times 7 - 5 =$
14 $6 \times 4 + 120 =$
15 $25 \div 5 \times 10 =$
16 $5 \times 44 \div 22 =$
17 $14 + 50 \times 2 =$
18 $20 + 28 \div 12 =$
19 $35 \div 7 \div 5 =$
20 $50 - 7 \times 10 =$
21 $3 + 39 \times 5 =$
22 $6 \times 5 + 170 =$
23 $48 \div 12 - 2 =$

24	$3 + 15 \times 2 =$
25	$16 \times 3 + 25 =$
26	$10 + 8 \div 9 =$
27	$5 - 5 \times 27 =$
28	$2 \times 6 \times 5 =$
29	$1 \times 10 + 117 =$
30	$36 \div 9 \times 6 =$

Numerical Test 6 (Combination – Percentages and Fractions, Series, Equations)

This test brings together everything you have done so far, and asks you to apply it to more real world problems. The test that follows involves dealing with number series, percentages, fractions, decimals and equations. This test begins to introduce you to some numerical problem solving – it provides you with a range of possible answers from which you need to select the correct one. In some cases you can identify what the correct answer must be *without* having to do any actual calculation. Remember that fractions, decimals, algebra and percentages are all just the application of basic addition, subtraction, multiplication and division.

Because the answers in this type of test are sometimes given, you may not have to work out possible solutions from scratch. It is quite possible to simply insert one answer option after another (especially in the case of algebraic equations) until you find the correct one, or until you have exhausted them all without finding the correct one.

Type of test: Speed / Power

Typical length: 25–40 questions

Typical time allowed: 25–40 minutes

Used for: Intermediate / higher level

Frequency of use: Common

Answer the following questions, choosing the correct answer, if you think there is one, from the set of five response options below. You have 35 minutes.

1 Which number comes next in the following series?

   1   4   7   10   13   16

   a) 17   b) 19   c) 21   d) 25   e) none of these

2 What is p in this equation?

   $2 + 3p = 14$

   a) 2   b) 3   c) 4   d) 6   e) none of these

3 $0.2 \times 5 =$

   a) $1/2$ b) 0.75   c) 1   d) $1^1/_2$ e) none of these

4 $1/_4 \times 1/_2 =$

   a) $1/_{16}$ b) $1/_8$ c) 1   d) 2   e) none of these

5 15% of 200 =

   a) 15   b) 30   c) 45   d) 60   e) none of these

6 Which number comes next in this series?

   0   1   3   6   10   15

   a) 19   b) 21   c) 26   d) 32   e) none of these

7 $3x + 2y = 14$

   If x is 4 then what is y?

   a) –6   b) 1   c) 7   d) 12   e) none of these

8 $^{0.3}/_{0.2} + 1.5 =$

   a) 1   b) 1.6   c) 2.5   d) 3   e) none of these

9 Which number replaces z in this equation?

$3/4 - z/12 = 1/4$

a) 1   b) 2   c) 4   d) 6   e) none of these

10 50% of $200/100 =$

a) 0   b) 1   c) 2   d) 50   e) none of these

11 Which number comes next in this series?

0   1   –1   2   –2   3

a) –4   b) –3   c) 4   d) 5   e) none of these

12 What is m?

$m/4 = m - 6$

a) –2   b) 2   c) 4   d) 8   e) none of these

13 What number replaces k in this equation?

$(k \times 0.4) + k = 2.8$

a) 0.5   b) 1   c) 1.5   d) 2   e) none of these

14 $4/9 \times 3/6 =$

a) $2/9$ b) $6/18$ c) $2/3$ d) $1/9$ e) none of these

15 20% of 0.1 =

a) 1   b) 0.2   c) 0.02   d) 1.2   e) none of these

16 Which number comes next in this series?

1   1   2   3   5   8

a) 10   b) 12   c) 13   d) 15   e) none of these

17 $2y \times 2y =$

a) y b) $2y$ c) $2y^2$ d) $4y^2$ e) none of these

18 Which of the following is exactly divisible by 6.2?

a) 26.2   b) 43.4   c) 60.2   d) 160.2   e) none of these

19 $1 = \frac{1}{9} + \frac{16}{?}$

a) 9   b) 16   c) 18   d) 32   e) none of these

20 8 = 20% of:

a) 20   b) 40   c) 16   d) 160   e) none of these

21 Which number comes next in this series?

0   1   2   5   20   25

a) 50   b) 75   c) 125   d) 150   e) none of these

22 If $x = z$ and $z = 3$ then:

$\frac{x}{z} + x =$

a) 2   b) 3   c) 4   d) 6   e) none of these

23 $2.1 \times 2.1 - 0.75 =$

a) 1.21   b) 2.42   c) 3.66   d) 3.25   e) none of these

24 $\frac{1}{4} + \frac{1}{2} \times \frac{3}{4} =$

a) $\frac{3}{8}$ b) $\frac{9}{16}$ c) $\frac{12}{6}$ d) $\frac{1}{4}$ e) none of these

25 10% of 40% of 200 =

a) 8   b) 20   c) 40   d) 80   e) none of these

26 Which number comes next in this series?

1   1   0   –1   –1   –2

a) –3   b) –4   c) –5   d) 2   e) none of these

27 $6p + 4q = 2q + 2p$ is the same as:

    a) $2qp + 2 = 4$
    b) $4p + 2q = 0$
    c) $2qp + 2p = 4q$
    d) $4q + 2p = 0$
    e) none of these

28 Which number replaces t in this equation?

    $^{1.2}/_t = 1.2 + 3.64 - 4.84$

    a) 0.21   b) 0   c) 2.2   d) 2   e) none of these

29 $^3/_5$ of $^3/_8$ is:

    a) $^3/_{15}$ b) $^6/_{15}$ c) $^9/_8$ d) $^9/_{40}$ e) none of these

30 60% of 340 is greater than:

    a) 190   b) 220   c) 240   d) 260   e) none of these

Numerical Test 7 (Number Series)

So far we have seen examples of numerical tests that have tended to focus on mathematical ability, with a small amount of problem solving involved. Now we turn our attention to some more difficult numerical ability tests that expressly address problem solving – how well you can identify which mathematical calculations you need to perform in order to reach the correct answer.

It is less important in this type of test to be able to carry out straightforward mathematical calculations – the emphasis is on how you get to that point. Note again that as in Test 6 the actual mathematical calculations involved are sometimes quite simple once you know what they are.

Type of test: Speed/Power

Typical length: 15–25 questions

Typical time allowed: 20–30 minutes

Used for: Intermediate/higher level

Frequency of use: Not that common in this 'pure' form but items of this type crop up from time to time.

This test contains a set of number series, arranged in pairs with two numbers in each square. In this test your task is to look at the number in the top left diagonal of the square and work out how it relates to the number in the bottom right diagonal of the same square. There are five squares in each set and they all share the same rule for relating the top number to the bottom number. Occasionally you may come across a version of this test that asks you to identify the odd one out, rather than the next in the sequence. With this type of test, the principle and method of solving the question are identical.

When you have worked out what the rule is, you should be able to work out the missing number. Give yourself 25 minutes.

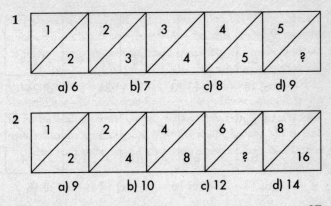

1

| 1 / | 2 / | 3 / | 4 / | 5 / |
| / 2 | / 3 | / 4 | / 5 | / ? |

   a) 6   b) 7   c) 8   d) 9

2

| 1 / | 2 / | 4 / | 6 / | 8 / |
| / 2 | / 4 | / 8 | / ? | / 16 |

   a) 9   b) 10   c) 12   d) 14

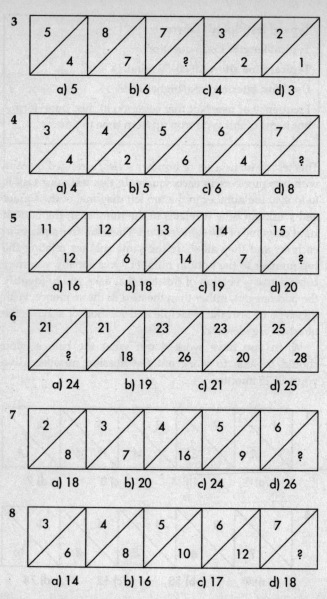

3

| 5 / 4 | 8 / 7 | 7 / ? | 3 / 2 | 2 / 1 |

a) 5 b) 6 c) 4 d) 3

4

| 3 / 4 | 4 / 2 | 5 / 6 | 6 / 4 | 7 / ? |

a) 4 b) 5 c) 6 d) 8

5

| 11 / 12 | 12 / 6 | 13 / 14 | 14 / 7 | 15 / ? |

a) 16 b) 18 c) 19 d) 20

6

| 21 / ? | 21 / 18 | 23 / 26 | 23 / 20 | 25 / 28 |

a) 24 b) 19 c) 21 d) 25

7

| 2 / 8 | 3 / 7 | 4 / 16 | 5 / 9 | 6 / ? |

a) 18 b) 20 c) 24 d) 26

8

| 3 / 6 | 4 / 8 | 5 / 10 | 6 / 12 | 7 / ? |

a) 14 b) 16 c) 17 d) 18

28

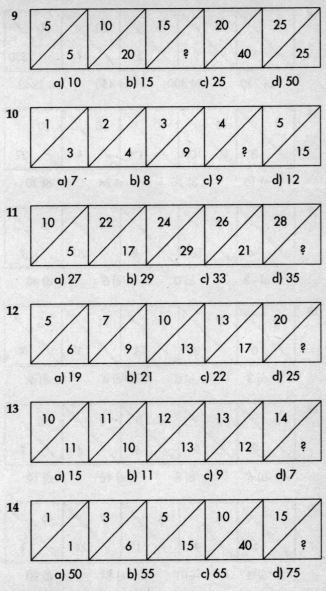

9

| 5 | 10 | 15 | 20 | 25 |
| 5 | 20 | ? | 40 | 25 |

a) 10 b) 15 c) 25 d) 50

10

| 1 | 2 | 3 | 4 | 5 |
| 3 | 4 | 9 | ? | 15 |

a) 7 b) 8 c) 9 d) 12

11

| 10 | 22 | 24 | 26 | 28 |
| 5 | 17 | 29 | 21 | ? |

a) 27 b) 29 c) 33 d) 35

12

| 5 | 7 | 10 | 13 | 20 |
| 6 | 9 | 13 | 17 | ? |

a) 19 b) 21 c) 22 d) 25

13

| 10 | 11 | 12 | 13 | 14 |
| 11 | 10 | 13 | 12 | ? |

a) 15 b) 11 c) 9 d) 7

14

| 1 | 3 | 5 | 10 | 15 |
| 1 | 6 | 15 | 40 | ? |

a) 50 b) 55 c) 65 d) 75

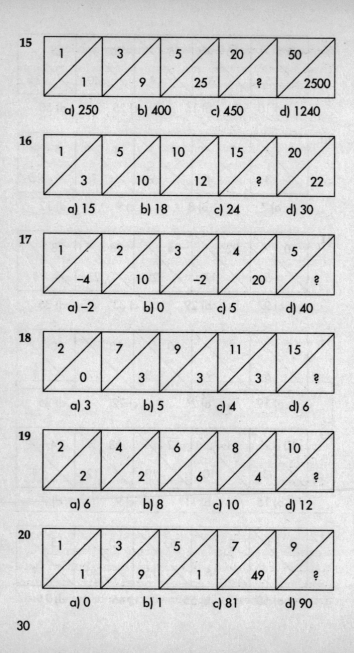

15

| 1 | 3 | 5 | 20 | 50 |
| 1 | 9 | 25 | ? | 2500 |

a) 250   b) 400   c) 450   d) 1240

16

| 1 | 5 | 10 | 15 | 20 |
| 3 | 10 | 12 | ? | 22 |

a) 15   b) 18   c) 24   d) 30

17

| 1 | 2 | 3 | 4 | 5 |
| −4 | 10 | −2 | 20 | ? |

a) −2   b) 0   c) 5   d) 40

18

| 2 | 7 | 9 | 11 | 15 |
| 0 | 3 | 3 | 3 | ? |

a) 3   b) 5   c) 4   d) 6

19

| 2 | 4 | 6 | 8 | 10 |
| 2 | 2 | 6 | 4 | ? |

a) 6   b) 8   c) 10   d) 12

20

| 1 | 3 | 5 | 7 | 9 |
| 1 | 9 | 1 | 49 | ? |

a) 0   b) 1   c) 81   d) 90

30

Numerical Tests 8 (Numerical Problem Solving)

These types of test are very commonly used in graduate and managerial selection, not least because they ask the test taker to apply their skills to deal with realistic problems in contexts that are expressly designed to approximate what actually happens in the workplace.

This test is almost a work sample. Pay particular attention to the fact that it requires no specialist financial or related knowledge. It samples the activities typically carried out by someone working with numerical information at a higher level, but does not need any more than a basic understanding of mathematical principles to complete. This is not at all like what one might expect from a marketing or accountancy qualifying exam – although it may look like one at first.

So please, if you see a test like this, do not be worried by it! At first glance the items look very complex and you will need to spend time understanding what is being asked of you. Do not worry if you don't come up with the answer in a few seconds, that is not what the test is designed to allow you to do.

Type of test: Classic Power Test

Typical length: 5–15 longer items, each with perhaps 5–10 questions relating to it

Typical time allowed: 35 minutes to one hour or longer

Used for: Higher level

Frequency of use: Very common in managerial or professional selection

---

Following are five separate tests numbered 1–5. Each has a number of sub-questions relating to that particular test. Your task is to choose which of the response options is the correct one. If you think none are correct then choose the option 'none of these'. Give yourself 45 minutes for all 5 tests.

1 The Telecom Company Limited provides international telephone calls for its customers. Its call charges in Euros per minute are shown below.

Customer Location			Call Destination
Germany	UK	France	
1.00	2.50	2.00	India
2.50	1.50	1.20	United States
2.00	2.00	1.00	Australia
2.00	3.00	2.50	Singapore

Call Cost

i) A ten minute call to the United States would be cheapest from which country?

a) Germany   b) UK   c) France

ii) A businessman travels regularly between Germany, France and the UK. He wishes to make a 5-minute call to each of India, the United States and Australia. Assuming he is free to choose which country he makes each of the calls from, what would be the least amount of money he could do it for?

a) 12.50   b) 14   c) 16   d) 16.70   e) none of these

iii) Which customer location has the cheapest average international call rates?

a) Germany   b) UK   c) France

iv) On average, over all customer locations, which is the most expensive destination country to call?

a) India   b) United States   c) Australia   d) Singapore

v) Assuming a 50% decrease in call charges after 6 pm local time, it is cheaper to call Singapore after 6 pm from the UK than it is to call India from France before 6 pm.

a) True   b) False

vi) Assuming a 50% decrease in call charges after 6 pm local time, how much would a call cost from

Germany to Singapore which commenced at 5.50 pm
and ended at 6.15 pm?

a) 20   b) 25   c) 35   d) 45   e) none of these

2   WorldWide CompSystems Ltd sell computer systems.
They have 3 different systems which are sold to 3 different categories of customer.

System 1 – is sold to individual consumers.
System 2 – is sold to distributors who sell them on
under their own name.
System 3 – is sold directly to businesses.

Below are the sales figures for each of the three systems for
the first two quarters of the current financial year.

	Jan		Feb		March		April		May		June	
	Units Sold	Sales Value	Units Sold	Sales Value	Units Sold	Sales Value	Units Sold	Sales Value	Units Sold	Sales Value	Units Sold	Sales Value
System 1	70	70k	100	100k	130	130k	160	160k	190	190k	210	210k
System 2	190	95k	200	100k	210	105k	220	110k	230	115k	240	120k
System 3	315	126k	320	128k	330	132k	345	138k	365	146k	390	150k

i) What is the cost per unit of System 1?

a) 900   b) 950   c) 1000   d) 1150

ii) What is the cost per unit of System 2?

a) 350   b) 450   c) 500   d) 560

iii) What is the cost per unit of System 3?

a) 270   b) 290   c) 400   d) 420

iv) What is the likely sales value in July for System 1?

a) 210k   b) 220k   c) 230k   d) 280k

v) What is the likely sales value in July for System 2?

a) 125k   b) 135k   c) 140k   d) 145k

vi) What is the likely sales value in July for System 3?

a) 155k   b) 158k   c) 164k   d) 168k

vii) What was the total sales income over all systems for the period Jan–March inclusive?

a) 868k   b) 896k   c) 968k   d) 986k

viii) What was the total number of units sold across the Systems 1 and 2 product range for January, February and April?

a) 860   b) 940   c) 980   d) 1060

ix) Taking all three systems together, what was the approximate average value per unit sold for April?

a) 100k   b) 250k   c) 480k   d) 600k

x) Which system has the most unit sales over the whole period?

a) System 1   b) System 2   c) System 3

xi) Which system generates most sales value over the second quarter?

a) System 1   b) System 2   c) System 3

3   On a certain date, a traveller from the UK intends to purchase foreign currency for a planned trip to a number of different countries in Europe. The exchange rates on the day they purchase their currency are shown below.

Our traveller has also calculated the living expenses for every whole day spent in each of the different countries.

Currency	£1.00 buys	Cost of living per day
Dutch Guilder	3.7	£50.00
French Franc	11	£75.00
German Mark	3.3	£50.00
Italian Lira	3250	£100.00
Belgian Franc	70	£110.00
Spanish Peseta	280	£75.00
Swedish Krona	15	£100.00
Swiss Franc	2.5	£50.00

i) If our traveller spends three days in each of Holland, Germany and Spain how much would they spend in total in Pounds Sterling?

a) £425.00 b) £475.00 c) £525.00 d) £575.00

ii) How much would 4½ days in Sweden cost in Pounds Sterling?

a) £350.00 b) £450.00 c) £475.00 d) £550.00

iii) If our traveller has to spend two days in each of three different countries, which three countries would represent the cheapest option?

a) Germany, France, Switzerland
b) Holland, Germany, Switzerland
c) France, Spain, Holland
d) Spain, Sweden, Germany

iv) Our traveller has decided that they will not spend more than £400.00 in total. Assuming they intend to spend at least one whole day in each of the countries they have decided to visit, what is the maximum number of countries they could visit?

a) 4 b) 5 c) 6 d) 7

v) How much would 2,200 French francs cost in Pounds Sterling?

a) £180.00 b) £200.00 c) £300.00 d) £400.00

vi) How many Belgian Francs could be bought for £550.00?

a) 2,850 b) 3,850 c) 38,500 d) 42,800

vii) How much would three days in Italy, two days in Switzerland and two days in Holland cost in Pounds Sterling?

a) £400.00 b) £450.00 c) £500.00 d) £575.00

viii) If our traveller had £650.00 to spend, could they afford to visit all eight countries spending at least one whole day in each?

a) Yes   b) No

ix) If our traveller bought 11,000 French Francs and 750 Swedish Krona, how much change would they have out of £1,250.00?

a) £150.00   b) £200.00   c) £250.00   d) £275.00

4   Software Delecon Inc. is deciding which of three servers it should use to distribute a single piece of software (size 100 Mb) to its many clients. It intends to post the software on a server, and invite clients to download it from the server themselves.

Each server is in a different country, has a different download speed (Mb per second), has a limitation in Mb on how much data can be downloaded per day (bandwidth) and bases its charges on how much data is downloaded per day (in Mb). This information is presented below.

Server	Location	Cost per 100 Mb	Download speed (Mb per sec)	Maximum bandwidth per day (Mb)
1	US	$100.00	1.2	1,200
2	UK	$120.00	2	1,000
3	Holland	$ 80.00	1.5	800

i) Which server provides the cheapest downloading costs?

a) Server 1   b) Server 2   c) Server 3

ii) Software Delecon Inc. expect clients to download their software at the rate of 11 units per day. Which server should they use to ensure their clients are not restricted in downloading the software due to bandwidth restrictions?

a) Server 1   b) Server 2   c) Server 3

iii) By how much should Software Delecon Inc. ask the US server to reduce its price per 100 Mb downloaded to bring the total cost of clients downloading 10 units per day to $800.00?

a) $10.00   b) $15.00   c) $20.00   d) $35.00

iv) The Dutch server provider increases its charges by 20%. Which server now provides the cheapest downloading costs?

a) Server 1   b) Server 2   c) Server 3

v) By using all three servers, how many software units could be downloaded in three days?

a) 20   b) 60   c) 90   d) 120

vi) Which server provides the quickest download speed for the least cost per 100 Mb?

a) Server 1   b) Server 2   c) Server 3

vii) How long would it take to download five pieces of software, one after the other, from the UK server?

a) 4 minutes 10 seconds
b) 4 minutes
c) 3 minutes 50 seconds
d) 1 hour 3 minutes

5   On the production line shown overleaf, the normal product failure rate is 2%. This means that for every 100 individual product units that come off the line, two will fail quality control.

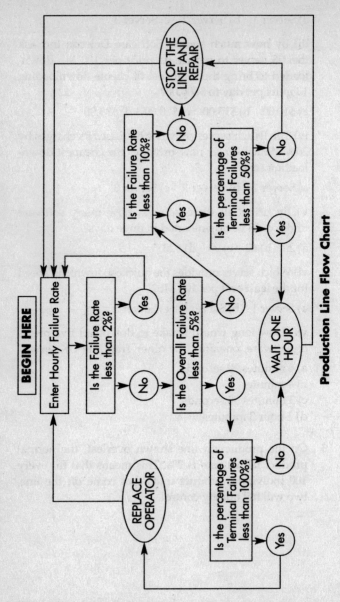

Production Line Flow Chart

BEGIN HERE

Enter Hourly Failure Rate

Is the Failure Rate less than 2%? → Yes
Is the Failure Rate less than 2%? → No → Is the Overall Failure Rate less than 5%?

Is the Overall Failure Rate less than 5%? → No → WAIT ONE HOUR
Is the Overall Failure Rate less than 5%? → Yes → Is the percentage of Terminal Failures less than 100%?

Is the percentage of Terminal Failures less than 100%? → Yes → REPLACE OPERATOR
Is the percentage of Terminal Failures less than 100%? → No → WAIT ONE HOUR

Is the Failure Rate less than 10%? → Yes → Is the percentage of Terminal Failures less than 50%?
Is the Failure Rate less than 10%? → No

Is the percentage of Terminal Failures less than 50%? → Yes → WAIT ONE HOUR
Is the percentage of Terminal Failures less than 50%? → No

STOP THE LINE AND REPAIR

38

Failures can be of two types – terminal, which means that the affected unit cannot be repaired cost effectively, and non-terminal, which means that the affected unit can be sent for repair. The Production Manager needs to consider two figures – firstly, the overall percentage failure rate, and secondly, what percentage of that rate is accounted for by terminal failures.

A high overall percentage hourly failure rate (i.e. higher than 10%) usually means that there is a serious problem with the production line (most often caused by excess line feed) and that failure of the entire line is imminent.

An overall percentage hourly failure rate of 5% or less is usually due to individual operator error – in these cases the operator can usually be replaced in order to rectify the problem and bring the failure rate back down to below 2%. This is the case even if the total terminal failure rate is higher than it would be in the case of excess line feed.

The decision-making process used by the Production Manager in deciding what to do when faced with product failures is shown below.

i) How many outcomes, denoted by large ovals, are possible in this chart?

a) 2   b) 3   c) 4   d) 5

ii) An overall failure rate of less than 5% will result in the line being stopped.

a) True   b) False

iii) From how many direct sources can the decision to stop the line for repairs come?

a) 2   b) 3   c) 4   d) 5

iv) If the hourly failure rate is 4%, with 75% of that being due to terminal failures, what is the outcome?

a) Replace operator
b) Wait one hour

c) Stop line for repair
d) None of these

v) If the hourly failure rate is 9%, with 25% of that being due to terminal failures, what is the outcome?

a) Replace operator
b) Wait one hour
c) Stop line for repair
d) None of these

vi) If the hourly failure rate is 12%, with 15% of that being due to terminal failures, what is the outcome?

a) Replace operator
b) Wait one hour
c) Stop line for repair
d) None of these

vii) If the hourly failure rate is 2%, with 25% of that being due to terminal failures, what is the outcome?

a) Replace operator
b) Wait one hour
c) Stop line for repair
d) None of these

OTHER TYPES OF NUMERICAL TESTS

If an organization is interested in your numerical ability, then it makes sense to use a test that gets as close to that ability as possible with a minimum of complexity. This means that while there are quite a few test publishers, there are relatively few formats of numerical tests on the market. Numerical ability is quite well defined and there is not much you can do with it other than what you have already seen in this chapter.

Occasionally, you may come across tests using a more unusual format. While still measuring numerical ability, these can take a bit more thought to work out exactly what a particular question means. One such format is the grid series. Some examples are shown below.

Example 1

The numerical values contained in the topmost row of cells and those in the leftmost row of cells combine in some way to produce the values a–g in the remaining cells. Identify the basis for this combination and work out the values in the remaining cells.

	4	6	8
4	16	a	b
6	c	d	e
8	f	g	64

In this case, all of the information you require in order to complete the question is given to you. The key is in the value '16'. The only possible way that 4 and 4 can combine to produce 16 is by using multiplication – and to confirm this the lower right cell contains the value '64', which can only be produced by multiplying 8 by 8. Solving the remainder of the question is straightforward. The full solution is given below.

	4	6	8
4	16	24	32
6	24	36	48
8	32	48	64

A slightly different example is shown below. In this case, not only are some of the answer cells empty, but so too are some of the cells on the topmost row and leftmost row of cells.

Example 2

The numerical values contained in the topmost row of cells and those in the leftmost row of cells combine in some way to produce the values in the remaining cells.

Identify the basis for this combination and work out the values in the remaining cells.

	a	b	9
3	9	18	d
5	15	e	f
c	21	42	63

The key here is to be systematic. Once again start with the first combination value, in this case the value 9. The table tells us that we need to do something with the number 3, and another number a in order to produce a value of 9.

Let's begin by trying $3 + 6 = 9$, which would make the value of a equal to 6. Unfortunately, 6 x 5 does not give us 15, so we start again.

This time let's try $3 \times 3 = 9$, which would make the value of a equal to 3. This fits in with $5 \times 5 = 15$. Furthermore, when we test our theory that multiplication is what we are about, we see that 9 x 7 produces the answer of 63, and 3 x 7 produces the answer of 21. The remainder of the questions are solved the same way – trying a number, applying some rule to it, and then testing it with another known outcome. This is the same whether the action required is addition, subtraction, multiplication or division. The full solution is given below.

	3	6	9
3	9	18	27
5	15	30	45
7	21	42	63

Occasionally you may come across a version of the number grid which requires you to work out what is being done with the numbers contained in the grid in order to produce a specific outcome, rather than having to try and identify the numbers themselves.

Example 3

What are the mathematical operators (signs) that replace the letters *a–l* in the grid below?

1	a	3	b	4
c		d		e
3	f	1	g	2
h		i		j
4	k	2	l	6

The correct answer is given below.

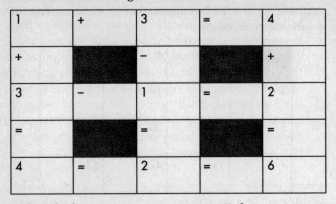

1	+	3	=	4
+		–		+
3	–	1	=	2
=		=		=
4	=	2	=	6

Although these test formats are not all that common, it pays to be familiar with them. The best way to practise is to try and design your own – they can be as sophisticated or difficult as you wish to make them.

Later in this book you will come across tests which ask you to do things like check columns of numbers for errors. While tests such as these look numerical in nature, the content is really irrelevant – they require no real mathematical ability and are, in fact, tests of perceptual speed and accuracy. This is why they are not included in this chapter.

HINTS ON DEALING WITH NUMERICAL TESTS

- The correct answer is usually amongst the answer options presented. This is to give you the chance to show that you know how the question is solved, rather than just guessing. If you are given a 'none of these' answer option, then you know the correct answer may not be among those you have been presented with.
- You may or may not be allowed to use a calculator, take one along just in case. If this isn't mentioned in the administration instructions, check with the administrator before using it.

- Don't be blinded by science – a seemingly complex problem is seldom as complex as it seems. Always try to break down a question into its component parts. Remember that at a fundamental level you will still be carrying out quite simple mathematical operations. In Numerical Test 8 in this chapter you were implicitly invited to look at the whole question and think 'that's too complicated – I will never solve this!' In reality, the specific questions you were then asked only demanded that you focus on a few specific aspects of the information you were presented with at once.

Many people freeze when faced with numbers, especially if they are in a form that they are not used to, so bear in mind some basics:

- Work carefully and systematically.
- With any number near 10 or a multiple of 10, it may be easier to treat it as 10 then add or subtract. You can do the same with 5 or with a number ending with a 2, 5 or 0.
- You can also estimate the correct answer by its size, for instance:

$120 \times 34,000$ must have a solution that is approximately seven digits long, so out of the possible answers:

a) 4080   b) 48,000   c) 840,000   d) 4,080,000

one can realistically estimate that d) must be the correct answer. If you are given the answer option 'none of these', then you need to be careful about using this short cut – the number of digits may be correct but the actual answer may not be. Tests that ask you to estimate numerical amounts tend not to have this answer option.

- Try rounding numbers up or down to the nearest zero. For instance, 97 x 9 is quite difficult to work out, but 97 x 10 is much easier and gives 970, and you can then subtract 97 to get the answer.

Remember your basic arithmetic from school (if you can remember back that far!). The following basic rules hold true whether you are dealing with number based problems, or algebra based problems:

- A negative number is still a number, e.g. an answer of –5 is quite valid.
- A percentage is simply a decimal – 20% of 100 is the same as 0.20 x 100.
- A decimal is also the same as a fraction, $1/4$ is the same as $(1 \div 4)$. So, $1/2$ x 10 is the same as $(1 \div 2)$ x 10, and 0.5 x 10.
- A minus multiplied by a minus always equals a plus (for instance, –5 x –5 = 25).
- A minus multiplied by a plus always equals a minus (for instance, –4 x 2 = –8).
- A division based problem can always be turned into a multiplication based one (for instance, a ÷ b = z, is the same as a = b x z). This is very useful and can be used to solve percentage based problems as follows:

  20% of a = 100, is the same as 0.2 x a = 100, which can be written as $a = {}^{100}/_{0.2}$. Applying a little more basic maths we can multiply both the bottom number (the denominator of this fraction) by 10 to make it a whole number (not forgetting to do the same with the top number – the numerator) to keep the ratio of top to bottom number equal. This gives us ${}^{1000}/_2 = 500$.

- With a calculation involving numbers or figures contained within brackets, always try to calculate whatever is contained within the brackets first. For instance:

  $(4 \times z) + 4z = ?$

When you calculate (4 x z) first you then get

$4z + 4z = ?$

which makes the solution of 8z simpler to arrive at.

- Sometimes working a bracketed figure out the long way can assist you in seeing what is being described:

  $4(a + b)$ is the same as $4a + 4b$

  On the other hand, doing the same backwards can be of help:

  $5y + 5z$ is the same as $5(y + z)$

  This rule works for addition and subtraction tasks within brackets. It does not work with multiplication or division!

- For number sequences you must systematically begin to apply both an operation to the number in question (multiply, add, subtract or divide) and another value to perform the operation on. So in the case of:

  1   2   4   8   16

  First we try adding 1, 2, 3, 4, and find that adding 1 helps but doesn't solve the next value. So then we try multiplying by 1, 2, 3, 4 and so on without success. Subtracting 2 doesn't help either – it solves the second value but not the first. But multiplying each value by 2 produces the correct sequence.

- With number series, your task is to find the correct combination of both value and operation. Remember that the value can be negative as well as positive and that both numerical values, direction (positive or negative), and the operation can vary so you could find a combination of 'divide by –1, add 1, divide by –2, add 1, divide by –3 add 1', and so on. The trick is to start simply at first, then add in combinations, first of number values then of operators (the signs +, x, – and ÷).

3

Tests of Verbal Ability

As with numerical ability, verbal ability tests can be divided into tests of simple verbal ability, which examine a person's basic verbal skills, and tests of verbal reasoning that look at how well a person can apply their verbal skills to solve more complex problems. This is sometimes known as critical thinking.

Verbal tests usually cover spelling, word use or comprehension, and grammar. As with numerical ability, you may be faced with individual tests that focus on one specific aspect of verbal ability, or, more commonly, with one that includes questions relating to a number of different verbal areas. This could be a series of sentences containing spelling or comprehension errors, your task being to locate them. They all still depend on basic spelling ability.

Verbal Test 1 (Spelling)

> **Type of test:** Speed
> **Typical length:** 25–40 questions
> **Typical time allowed:** 20–30 minutes
> **Used for:** Basic level
> **Frequency of use:** Common

Your task here is quite simple. Choose which of the set of four words is spelt correctly. If you think none of them are spelt correctly, then choose option (e). Give yourself 25 minutes.

1 Which of these words is spelt correctly?

a) Extraeneous
b) Extranious
c) Extraneous
d) Extraineous
e) none of these

2 Which of these words is spelt correctly?

a) Exuberant
b) Exubirant
c) Exuberint
d) Exubuerant
e) none of these

3 Which of these words is spelt correctly?

a) Phosphorece
b) Phospharesce
c) Phosphorecse
d) Phosphorese
e) none of these

4 Which of these words is spelt correctly?

a) Ordernance
b) Ordanance
c) Ordnence
d) Ordnance
e) none of these

5 Which of these words is spelt correctly?

a) Ettiquette
b) Etiquettue
c) Etiquette
d) Etiquete
e) none of these

6 Which of these words is spelt correctly?

a) Estrangment
b) Estrangiment
c) Estrangement
d) Estrangemant
e) none of these

7 Which of these words is spelt correctly?

a) Capillary
b) Cappillary
c) Cappilary
d) Capilary
e) none of these

8 Which of these words is spelt correctly?

a) Anarckism
b) Anarcism
c) Anarchasm
d) Anarchism
e) none of these

9 Which of these words is spelt correctly?

a) Harlequin
b) Harlequine
c) Harlaquin
d) Harliquin
e) none of these

10 Which of these words is spelt correctly?

a) Quadralatiral
b) Quadrelateral
c) Quadrilatiral
d) Quadralateral
e) none of these

11 Which of these words is spelt correctly?

a) Pyrotecnic
b) Pyrotecknic
c) Pyrotecnich
d) Pyrotechnic
e) none of these

12 Which of these words is spelt correctly?

a) Characteristically
b) Characteristicaly
c) Characteristacally
d) Charactaristicaly
e) none of these

13 Which of these words is spelt correctly?

a) Abbreviated
b) Abreiviated
c) Abbrieviated
d) Abrieviated
e) none of these

14 Which of these words is spelt correctly?

a) Coroborated
b) Corroborrated
c) Corrobarated
d) Corobborated
e) none of these

15 Which of these words is spelt correctly?

a) Conscioussness
b) Consciousnes
c) Consciousiness
d) Consciousines
e) none of these

16 Which of these words is spelt correctly?

a) Substansiated
b) Substantiated
c) Substaintiated
d) Subsantiated
e) none of these

17 Which of these words is spelt correctly?

a) Wherabouts
b) Wereabouts
c) Werabouts
d) Whereabouts
e) none of these

18 Which of these words is spelt correctly?

a) Alleviated
b) Allieviated
c) Alleiviated
d) Aleviated
e) none of these

19 Which of these words is spelt correctly?

a) Precident
b) Presedent
c) Prescedent
d) Precedent
e) none of these

20   Which of these words is spelt correctly?

   a) Improbabillity
   b) Improbibility
   c) Improbbability
   d) Improbibillity
   e) none of these

21   Which of these words is spelt correctly?

   a) Jambore
   b) Jamborree
   c) Jamborre
   d) Jamboree
   e) none of these

22   Which of these words is spelt correctly?

   a) Omniscient
   b) Onmiscient
   c) Omnisient
   d) Omnicient
   e) none of these

23   Which of these words is spelt correctly?

   a) Restarateur
   b) Restauranteur
   c) Restauratur
   d) Restaurater
   e) none of these

24   Which of these words is spelt correctly?

   a) Malevolence
   b) Malevolance
   c) Maelevolence
   d) Malevalence
   e) none of these

25 Which of these words is spelt correctly?

a) Convilution
b) Convolutian
c) Connvolution
d) Convolution
e) none of these

26 Which of these words is spelt correctly?

a) Decommpression
b) Decompression
c) Decompresion
d) Decommpresion
e) none of these

27 Which of these words is spelt correctly?

a) Matricuilate
b) Matrickulate
c) Matrikulate
d) Mattriculate
e) none of these

28 Which of these words is spelt correctly?

a) Lieutennant
b) Leiutenant
c) Leuitenant
d) Leuitennant
e) none of these

29 Which of these words is spelt correctly?

a) Gratuitious
b) Gratutous
c) Grattuitous
d) Gratuitus
e) none of these

30 Which of these words is spelt correctly?

  a) Omivorous
  b) Onmivorous
  c) Omnivorous
  d) Omnivorious
  e) none of these

31 Which of these words is spelt correctly?

  a) Underprivilleged
  b) Underprivileged
  c) Underpriveleged
  d) Underprivaleged
  e) none of these

32 Which of these words is spelt correctly?

  a) Electromagnatism
  b) Electramagnetism
  c) Electromagnitism
  d) Electromagnetism
  e) none of these

33 Which of these words is spelt correctly?

  a) Extinguised
  b) Extingushed
  c) Extinguished
  d) Extinuished
  e) none of these

34 Which of these words is spelt correctly?

  a) Fullfilment
  b) Fullfilmant
  c) Fullfillment
  d) Fulfillment
  e) none of these

35 Which of these words is spelt correctly?

a) Spontanious
b) Spontaineous
c) Spontaneous
d) Spontainious
e) none of these

36 Which of these words is spelt correctly?

a) Acuaintance
b) Acquaintaince
c) Acquantaince
d) Aquaintance
e) none of these

37 Which of these words is spelt correctly?

a) Denunciation
b) Denuntiation
c) Denuinciation
d) Denuncaition
e) none of these

38 Which of these words is spelt correctly?

a) Expeidience
b) Expediense
c) Expedience
d) Excpedience
e) none of these

39 Which of these words is spelt correctly?

a) Misdeameanour
b) Misdemenour
c) Misdemeanor
d) Misdemeanour
e) none of these

40 Which of these words is spelt correctly?

   a) Resourcfulness
   b) Resourcefullness
   c) Resoursefulness
   d) Resourcefulness
   e) none of these

Verbal Test 2 – Comprehension (Missing Words)

In this next test, your task is to read the sentence, then read the words underneath the sentence and decide which of those words, if any, would complete the sentence in such a way as to allow it to make most sense. Note here that often more than one word would satisfy this criterion, but what is being tested here is your ability to choose the word which makes most sense *in the context of the sentence it completes*. If you think that none of the words complete the sentence in such a way as to help it make sense then choose option (e).

> **Type of test:** Speed / Power
> **Typical length:** 20–30 questions
> **Typical time allowed:** 20–30 minutes
> **Used for:** Basic / Intermediate level
> **Frequency of use:** Common

Read each sentence and then read the words underneath that particular sentence and decide which of those words, if any, would complete the sentence in such a way as to allow it to make most sense. Give yourself 20 minutes.

1 After revising all week Paul finally felt --- for the exam.

   a) nervous   b) ready   c) revised   d) happy

2 He took the new lawn mower he had bought back to the shop --- that it wasn't working.

a) asking   b) repairing   c) wondering   d) complaining

3 Assembling the desk had been more difficult than he had ---.

a) done   b) assembled   c) imagined   d) tried

4 Answering telephones all day was not her idea of a --- job.

a) fulfilling   b) happy   c) steady   d) normal

5 She was disappointed that her new car did not start after it had been ---.

a) raining   b) fine   c) running   d) cleaned

6 He worked all day and all night to make sure his tax return was --- on time.

a) late   b) copied   c) accurate   d) completed

7 Looking at the clock, Brenda was --- to see that she had spent over two hours talking to her mother.

a) frightened   b) late   c) surprised   d) calm

8 He bought a new record from his local store and rushed --- to play it.

a) away   b) up   c) out   d) home

9 Mobile telephones were --- he had never quite managed to work out.

a) never   b) always   c) something   d) easy

10 Not wanting to upset her father, she left work early to ensure she would be in time for his --- birthday party.

a) surprise   b) own   c) latest   d) happy

11 The two of them went fishing, and although he felt guilty about missing work, John --- himself nonetheless.

a) hated   b) surprised   c) delayed   d) enjoyed

12 No matter what he did, he could not get the photo-copier to work, --- he called out a repairman.

a) yesterday   b) never   c) always   d) eventually

13 He met his wife, they had a meal and --- they went to the concert.

a) sickly   b) together   c) today   d) wondering

14 After visiting the gym for the first time, she felt she would not be too --- about going along again.

a) tired   b) fit   c) embarrassed   d) overdressed

15 The children had been misbehaving all day, she decided she had had enough of --- for other people.

a) looking   b) babysitting   c) waiting   d) smiling

16 The dog looked at him excitedly, --- Paul pulled on his coat and took his pet out for a walk in the rain.

a) reluctantly   b) excitedly   c) cold   d) generally

17 He had applied for the job some two weeks earlier, but had still not --- anything.

a) done   b) waited   c) lost   d) heard

18 He was not the best cook in the world but all his guests agreed that his chilli was the best they had --- for a long time.

a) served   b) tasted   c) bought   d) cooked

19 Caught in the rain, his new shoes had been --- beyond repair.

a) wet   b) worn   c) old   d) damaged

20 Painting was not his favourite pastime, but he --- to spend the whole weekend getting the decorating finished.

a) hated   b) resolved   c) painted   d) waited

Verbal Test 3 – Comprehension (Related Words)

Again this test measures your ability to understand word meanings and to complete a set of questions requiring you to apply that knowledge. Your task here is to establish what the relationship is between two words and then apply that knowledge to one other word and decide which word goes with it from one of a series which follow. Many of the questions are based on common or slang expressions rather than what one might consider 'proper' English. For this reason many such tests are highly culturally specific.

> **Type of test:** Speed/Power
>
> **Typical length:** 20–30 questions
>
> **Typical time allowed:** 20–30 minutes
>
> **Used for:** Basic/Intermediate level
>
> **Frequency of use:** Common

Which word completes a well-known phrase in conjunction with each of the other two? Give yourself 25 minutes.

1 blast --- set

a) off   b) smash   c) rare   d) grab   e) none of these

2 shook --- standing

a) off   b) down   c) up   d) barely   e) none of these

3 hand --- down

a) shake   b) tool   c) take   d) pin   e) none of these

4 telephone --- back

a) message   b) answer   c) right   d) call   e) none of these

5 watch --- off

a) out   b) face   c) hand   d) see   e) none of these

6 back --- handle

a) door   b) off   c) wing   d) up   e) none of these

7 key --- game

a) set   b) stone   c) win   d) board   e) none of these

8 motor --- port

a) car   b) race   c) ship   d) sea   e) none of these

9 right --- down

a) side   b) up   c) pick   d) take   e) none of these

10 washing --- tool

a) day   b) up   c) machine   d) hand   e) none of these

11 book --- up

a) shelf   b) cover   c) page   d) burn   e) none of these

12 piggy --- vault

a) deep   b) pen   c) bank   d) pole   e) none of these

13 toilet --- cage

a) door   b) bar   c) page   d) burn   e) none of these

14 horror --- theatre

    a) shock b) cover c) play d) ticket e) none of these

15 boxing --- fence

    a) match b) clever c) canvas d) ring e) none of these

16 milk --- ache

    a) tooth b) cow c) belly d) head e) none of these

17 musical --- girder

    a) note b) box c) iron d) bridge e) none of these

18 motor --- certainty

    a) engine b) never c) racing d) day e) none of these

19 legal --- general

    a) speak b) document c) in d) secretary e) none of these

20 compact --- drive

    a) disk b) mower c) house d) power e) none of these

21 fishing --- up

    a) rod b) wind c) trip d) catch e) none of these

22 water --- over

    a) down b) fall c) trip d) flow e) none of these

23 sticky --- recorder

    a) situation b) tape c) court d) video e) none of these

24 bowling --- fingers

a) over   b) five   c) green   d) quick   e) none of these

25 zebra --- point

a) marking   b) crossing   c) match   d) hidden   e) none of these

---

Verbal Test 4 – Comprehension (Related Words)

In this test you have to identify which of the words from the set of four is the odd one out. This requires you apply what you know about the real world. Some of the items are quite simple but others are more complex and can take a considerable time to solve.

For instance, in the set of words:

Blue   Red   Brown   Rock

the answer is quite simple. 'Rock' is the odd one out because the others are all colours. However, in the case of:

Clock   Whisk   Microwave   Scissors

it may take a little longer to realize that Microwave is the odd one out because the others can all be non-electrical devices while a Microwave cannot. You may have to try three or more potential solutions before you arrive at the correct answer. For instance, you may have decided that a clock was the only thing that one might not use exclusively in the kitchen, or scissors are the only item you can use to cut things. However, as these solutions are quite tenuous, the clearest answer is 'Microwave'.

Type of test: Speed/Power
Typical length: 25–40 questions
Typical time allowed: 25–35 minutes
Used for: Basic/Intermediate level
Frequency of use: Common

Which word in each set of four is the odd one out? Give yourself 30 minutes.

1 a) look   b) see   c) watch   d) face
   e) none

2 a) throw   b) catch   c) fling   d) cast
   e) none

3 a) never   b) then   c) today   d) now
   e) none

4 a) box   b) bag   c) crate   d) basket
   e) none

5 a) pain   b) anger   c) happiness d) fury
   e) none

6 a) read   b) newspaper c) letter   d) book
   e) none

7 a) paint   b) portrait   c) sketch   d) draw
   e) none

8 a) desk   b) chair   c) stool   d) sofa
   e) none

9 a) house   b) shed   c) garage   d) home
   e) none

10 a) bright b) lively   c) brilliant d) gleaming
   e) none

11 a) run   b) mile   c) stride   d) walk
   e) none

12 a) tape   b) tack   c) stick   d) glue
   e) none

13 a) error   b) mistake   c) slip   d) blunder
   e) none

14 a) bicycle b) motorbike c) car   d) bus
   e) none

15 a) loud   b) racket   c) din   d) bang
   e) none

16	a) river	b) stream	c) brook	d) beck
	e) none			
17	a) sleep	b) nap	c) doze	d) slumber
	e) none			
18	a) dog	b) cat	c) lion	d) rabbit
	e) none			
19	a) play	b) joy	c) frolic	d) romp
	e) none			
20	a) cool	b) chilly	c) bitter	d) snow
	e) none			
21	a) cod	b) carp	c) frog	d) goldfish
	e) none			
22	a) blue	b) red	c) colour	d) white
	e) none			
23	a) talk	b) shout	c) call	d) whistle
	e) none			
24	a) second	b) hour	c) minute	d) era
	e) none			
25	a) lamp	b) bulb	c) torch	d) bright
	e) none			

Verbal Test 5 – Comprehension (Related Words)

This test requires you to identify the relationship between two words e.g. *wheel* and *turn* and apply that information to a third word in order to identify its partner. This is similar to Test 4 in that you are looking for characteristics of the things the word describes rather than some physical or textual aspect of it. Because answering the questions involves a significant degree of problem solving (devising a rule and then testing it), this type of test can be more difficult than it looks.

Type of test: Speed / Power
Typical length: 25–35 questions
Typical time allowed: 30–35 minutes
Used for: Intermediate / Higher level
Frequency of use: Common

Give yourself 25 minutes.

1   Wheel is to turn as flame is to ---
    a) burn   b) hot   c) glow   d) light   e) none of these

2   Shoe is to foot as sock is to ---
    a) wind   b) hand   c) foot   d) leg   e) none of these

3   Wind is to blow as water is to ---
    a) flow   b) cold   c) wet   d) drink   e) none of these

4   Wood is to tree as feather is to ----
    a) down   b) light   c) bird   d) soft   e) none of these

5   Electricity is to bulb as wind is to ---
    a) windmill   b) flag   c) blow   d) turn   e) none of these

6   Hot is to sweat as cold is to ---
    a) snow   b) chilly   c) ice   d) shiver   e) none of these

7   Grass is to green as sky is to ---
    a) bright   b) blue   c) cloud   d) clear   e) none of these

8   Money is to bank as library is to ---
    a) borrow   b) local   c) read   d) book   e) none of these

9 Doctor is to patient as mechanic is to ---

a) car   b) fix   c) repair   d) damage   e) none of these

10 Blood is to heart as water is to ---

a) beat   b) red   c) pump   d) flow   e) none of these

11 Eat is to food as drink is to ---

a) water   b) dry   c) consume   d) thirst   e) none of these

12 Touch is to feel as look is to ---

a) eye   b) focus   c) hand   d) see   e) none of these

13 Ink is to pen as paint is to ---

a) art   b) picture   c) colour   d) canvas   e) none of these

14 Careless is to careful as happy is to ---

a) sad   b) smile   c) loose   d) cheery   e) none of these

15 Cow is to farm as dog is to ---

a) bark   b) puppy   c) cat   d) collar   e) none of these

16 Teacher is to classroom as judge is to ---

a) police   b) court   c) law   d) lawyer   e) none of these

17 Beach is to coast as mountain is to ---

a) snow   b) climb   c) rock   d) tall   e) none of these

18 Sleep is to bed as drive is to ---

a) passenger   b) tired   c) walk   d) car   e) none of these

19 Circle is to sphere as square is to ---

  a) round b) corner c) cube d) line e) none of these

20 Number is to count as letter is to ---

  a) read b) word c) book d) sentence e) none of these

Verbal Test 6 – Comprehension (Synonyms and Antonyms)

A synonym is a word that means the same as another word, while an antonym is a word that means the opposite of another word. You need to be careful that in the rush to complete the test you do not get the two mixed up.

> **Type of test:** Speed / Power
> **Typical length:** 25–35 questions
> **Typical time allowed:** 30–35 minutes
> **Used for:** Intermediate level
> **Frequency of use:** Common

Give yourself 25 minutes.

1 Pride is the opposite of ---

  a) humility b) proud c) suffer d) lion e) none of these

2 Relaxed means the same as the opposite of ---

  a) calm b) angry c) tense d) sleep e) none of these

3 Delve means the same as ---

  a) dig b) leave c) deep d) run e) none of these

4 Reject is the opposite of ---

  a) ban b) accept c) take d) leave e) none of these

5 Pursue means the same as ---

a) leaf   b) chase   c) harass   d) meander   e) none of these

6 Transparent is the opposite of ---

a) mask   b) cover   c) clear   d) opaque   e) none of these

7 Chaos means the opposite of the opposite of ---

a) disorder   b) organize   c) steady   d) predictable   e) none of these

8 Discrete means the same as ---

a) single   b) cautious   c) fixed   d) exude   e) none of these

9 Thaw is the opposite of ---

a) freeze   b) dissolve   c) melt   d) spring   e) none of these

10 Hidden means the opposite of the opposite of ---

a) concealed   b) hide   c) show   d) obvious   e) none of these

11 Scrupulous is the opposite of ---

a) careful   b) haste   c) clean   d) lazy   e) none of these

12 Conceit means the same as ---

a) show   b) pride   c) display   d) humble   e) none of these

13 Exclude means the same as the opposite of ---

a) leave   b) ban   c) reject   d) include   e) none of these

14 Intelligible means the same as ---

a) understandable   b) confusing   c) clever   d) smart
e) none of these

15 Legacy means the same as ---

a) donation   b) history   c) walking   d) hallmark
e) none of these

16 Delirious means the same as ---

a) happy   b) erasable   c) drunk   d) demented
e) none of these

17 Demise means the same as ---

a) clear   b) death   c) split   d) birth   e) none of these

18 Malign means the opposite of the opposite of ---

a) ill   b) regret   c) tolerate   d) accuse   e) none of
these

19 Reinforce is the opposite of ---

a) weaken   b) strengthen   c) strongest   d) tough
e) none of these

20 Transmit means the same as ---

a) carry   b) change   c) talk   d) save   e) none of
these

21 Clarify is the opposite of ---

a) clearer   b) confuse   c) murky   d) melt   e) none
of these

22 Assertive is the opposite of ---

a) challenge   b) fight   c) submit   d) aggression
e) none of these

23 Pilfer means the same as ---

a) nibble b) scan c) generous d) steal e) none of these

24 Labyrinth means the same as ---

a) maze b) solve c) historical d) confusing e) none of these

25 Profound is the opposite of ---

a) meaning b) discovered c) simple d) deep e) none of these

Verbal Test 7 – Problem Solving (Critical Thinking)

This type of test is quite commonly used in higher-level testing (such as managerial or graduate) and can require some careful thought as to what the correct answer is. Unlike the higher-level numerical tests we saw in the previous chapter, the correct answer here is not one which is always clearly so.

> **Type of test:** Classic Verbal Power Test
>
> **Typical length:** 5–15 longer items, each with perhaps 5–10 questions relating to it
>
> **Typical time allowed:** 35 minutes to one hour or longer
>
> **Used for:** Higher level
>
> **Frequency of use:** Very common in managerial or professional selection

In this next test there are five sets of information; each is followed by a series of statements that relate to the information. Your task is to read the information given and then decide for each of the statements that follow, whether they are:

a) True – the statement is true, based on the information you have read.
b) False – the statement is untrue, based on the information you have read.
c) Can't say – it is impossible to say whether the statement is true or untrue, based on the information you have read.

Allow yourself 45 minutes

1   The thinking behind the single European currency is quite simple. Suppose that a company in Germany wanted to buy some raw materials from a company in Spain. At the moment there is one major problem in them doing so.

   The exchange rate between the German mark and the Spanish peseta is variable. If the German company agreed to buy from the Spanish company Dm 5,000,000 worth of product over the course of a year, but had to invoice the amount in its peseta equivalent, a subsequent fluctuation in the exchange rate which made the German mark worth less in peseta terms could mean the German company ends up paying a lot more than it had originally intended.

   If both companies traded in the single European currency, the Euro, then such fluctuations in national currency exchange rates would have no effect. This greatly helps with business planning and cash flow.

   i) Most companies in Germany trade with companies in Spain.

   a) true   b) false   c) can't say

   ii) Fluctuations in exchange rates make financial planning difficult.

   a) true   b) false   c) can't say

   iii) Trading in the Euro means that fluctuations in exchange rates have no effect.

a) true   b) false   c) can't say

iv) German companies are more efficient than Spanish companies.

a) true   b) false   c) can't say

v) Business planning is essential for business success.

a) true   b) false   c) can't say

vi) Companies in Germany may want to trade with companies in Spain.

a) true   b) false   c) can't say

vii) The Euro is a good idea.

a) true   b) false   c) can't say

viii) Things are cheaper in Spain than in Germany.

a) true   b) false   c) can't say

ix) The arguments in favour of the Euro are complex.

a) true   b) false   c) can't say

x) It is expensive to move goods from Spain to Germany.

a) true   b) false   c) can't say

2   Greenhouses are one of those distinctly British things. Many gardens have them, and they can come in a variety of shapes and styles.

The commonest has to be the aluminium type. These can be bought as self-assembly packs from DIY and garden centres (the glass is usually sold separately), and can be built by a person with an average degree of DIY skill in about a day.

Less common are the wooden types. These tend not to last the worst of the British weather as well as the aluminium types do, but are far more pleasing on the eye.

Because the aluminium types tend to have far more glass than their wooden cousins, most people opt for Perspex windows, which, as well as being cheaper than glass, are also much tougher and, importantly, safer. The wooden types usually have glass rather than Perspex windows, mainly because they tend to be older and were built when Perspex was not as cheap and easily available as it is now.

i) Perspex is safer than glass.

a) true   b) false   c) can't say

ii) Only the British have greenhouses.

a) true   b) false   c) can't say

iii) There are fewer wooden greenhouses than aluminium greenhouses.

a) true   b) false   c) can't say

iv) The British love gardening.

a) true   b) false   c) can't say

v) DIY and garden centres only sell aluminium greenhouses.

a) true   b) false   c) can't say

vi) There are fewer wooden greenhouses than aluminium greenhouses because people like them less.

a) true   b) false   c) can't say

vii) Perspex is cheap.

a) true   b) false   c) can't say

viii) Anybody can assemble an aluminium greenhouse.

a) true   b) false   c) can't say

ix) A greenhouse is best for growing delicate plants.

a) true   b) false   c) can't say

x) Wooden greenhouses tend to be painted green.

a) true   b) false   c) can't say

3   After a decline lasting many years, the numbers of wild salmon re-entering English rivers is on the increase again. There are numerous reasons why the decline may have happened. Some blame the increasing wild seal population, for which the salmon is a major food source.

Some blame a rise in ocean temperatures, which we know can affect wild salmon behaviour. Others blame river pollution because it would seem to be the case that as pollution on our rivers has been reduced, then so has a rise occurred in the numbers of wild salmon returning to our rivers to spawn. A few people blame anglers, but the offshore netting industry, although not growing, takes far more fish than anglers do and some anglers have even banded together to buy up the offshore netting rights to remove at least this hazard to the returning salmon.

Anglers in Scotland, on the other hand, have only benefited from this whole affair, with increasing numbers of English anglers venturing north of the border to fish. Now that the fish are returning to English rivers, the income gained from visiting anglers in Scotland is set to fall.

i) This is not the first time salmon numbers have declined and then recovered.

a) true   b) false   c) can't say

ii) More fish are being caught in offshore nets now than were before.

a) true   b) false   c) can't say

iii) The wild seal population has been increasing.

a) true   b) false   c) can't say

iv) The salmon is the main food source for wild seals.

a) true   b) false   c) can't say

v) The Scottish economy depends on visiting anglers.

a) true   b) false   c) can't say

vi) As river pollution in England has decreased, then so have salmon numbers returning to the rivers.

a) true   b) false   c) can't say

vii) The salmon return to freshwater to spawn.

a) true   b) false   c) can't say

viii) There are more rivers in England than there are in Scotland.

a) true   b) false   c) can't say

ix) Anglers have been doing nothing to improve the situation.

a) true   b) false   c) can't say

x) Only male salmon return to rivers to spawn.

a) true   b) false   c) can't say

4   Older cars use more petrol, or so the argument goes. Campaigners have been arguing for some years that older cars should be scrapped when they reach the age of 20 years, by law. This has caused anger in the classic car world in which older cars are things to be preserved not scrapped.

While it is possible to see the point of classic car enthusiasts, namely that older cars are of historic value, one cannot deny that they are more damaging to the environment. Nonetheless, the numbers of people owning classic cars is on the increase. This is evidenced by the fact that 4-star leaded petrol can now be bought from selected petrol stations after not being available for many years. In the year 2000, some 22 million litres were authorized for release to the public by the government. This was a relief to the classic car world since some older cars cannot run on unleaded petrol without serious engine damage.

The pollution argument can only be overcome if more classic car owners use petrol additives which can be added to unleaded fuel and provide the same characteristics as leaded petrol without damaging the vehicle's engine or the environment.

i) Cars over 20 years old are not worth keeping.

a) true   b) false   c) can't say

ii) From now on 22 million litres of leaded petrol will be available to the public every year.

a) true   b) false   c) can't say

iii) Classic car owners can now drive their older cars without damaging the environment.

a) true   b) false   c) can't say

iv) Unleaded fuel damages the engines in all older cars.

a) true   b) false   c) can't say

v) Classic cars are interesting.

a) true   b) false   c) can't say

vi) Modern cars do not damage the environment.

a) true   b) false   c) can't say

vii) Campaigners say that only cars of 20 years or older, which have historic value, should not be scrapped.

a) true   b) false   c) can't say

viii) Petrol additives are very expensive.

a) true   b) false   c) can't say

ix) The number of people owning classic cars is not increasing.

a) true   b) false   c) can't say

x) Modern cars are lighter than older cars.

a) true   b) false   c) can't say

5 The 'Wheelie bin' is not a modern invention. They have been used in the United States for many years. Essentially, a Wheelie bin is a dustbin on wheels, with a hinged lid, which can be automatically emptied using a specially adapted waste disposal truck.

The advantages of Wheelie bins are that they are more hygienic than old dustbins, are easier to manoeuvre – for both the householder and the refuse collector – and they prevent animals such as cats and birds from scavenging through piles of rubbish bags.

On the other hand, many local authorities have not adopted them because of fears of redundancies in the local waste disposal services. Also, they require cleaning with powerful disinfectants, they are expensive, and they can be too large for the needs of those living alone or too unwieldy for the elderly to move about – although in recent years smaller and easier to handle bins have been designed.

i) Wheelie bins are more hygienic than dustbins.

a) true   b) false   c) can't say

ii) Older people prefer dustbins.

a) true   b) false   c) can't say

iii) Using Wheelie bins results in redundancies.

a) true   b) false   c) can't say

iv) Wheelie bins are quite inexpensive compared to dustbins.

a) true   b) false   c) can't say

v) Normal dustbin lorries can empty Wheelie bins.

a) true   b) false   c) can't say

vi) The elderly produce less waste than other people.

a) true   b) false   c) can't say

vii) People who live alone produce less waste than people who do not live alone.

a) true   b) false   c) can't say

viii) Wheelie bins can be wheeled around.

a) true   b) false   c) can't say

ix) Smaller Wheelie bins are less unwieldy than larger ones.

a) true   b) false   c) can't say

x) Dustbins do not need to be cleaned.

a) true   b) false   c) can't say

HINTS ON DEALING WITH VERBAL TESTS

In one sense, verbal tests are easier to deal with than numerical tests, mainly because we have been exposed to the subject matter from birth and we use it in our everyday lives. On the other hand, they can be trickier than something like a numerical test because the amount of potential subject matter is so large. Preparing for a verbal test can be tricky, so here are some useful tips to help you out.

Spelling Tests

When people read a word, they do not do it one letter at a time. Rather they 'see' the meaning of the word. For instance, when you read the word 'Decompression' you can take in its meaning in a much shorter time than you would if you read each single letter in turn and then tried to construct the word one letter at a time.

This means that, very often, the best strategy with spelling tests is to pick the answer that 'looks' right, and then to go through it letter by letter to check the spelling. This can be quite difficult since it is not what we are used to doing.

While there are certain spelling rules that we were taught at school (such as 'I' before 'E' except after 'C'), each has so many exceptions that they don't help much.

The items in the spelling test in this chapter are pretty representative of the type of items you will come across in a spelling test. They contain some of the common types of word that tend to crop up, such as words ending in 'tion', or with a series of 'ss' or 'ff' combinations. Examine them closely and try to find a similar word using a dictionary; when you find a similar word look to see what spelling rule they both have in common.

Spelling ability is something that is built up over time and the best way to do this is to read more challenging material than usual. Another method is to make a point of thinking about how you would spell the words you come across in every day life, perhaps by writing them down approximately and then looking up and writing down the correct spelling later.

If spelling is not one of your strong points, you are not alone. Next to numerical ability, it is the most dreaded type of test.

Missing Words

A similar process to reading individual words occurs when reading sentences where you have to fill in missing words. You should read the sentence as a whole and, without looking at the answers, then think what type of word would complete it. For instance in the case of:

It was a --- day so we all went to the beach

Without looking at any potential answers, you might think that the missing word described the weather rather than some other characteristic such as the length of the day, because the length of a day does not determine whether one goes to the beach.

However, sometimes you are presented with a version of a test that asks you to read a complete sentence and identify which word is out of place, such as:

I was relieved when the aeroplane finally took off after the long flight.

You may need to go through the sentence in fine detail, word by word, to identify the error (in this case the words 'took off' were wrong – planes do not take off after flights, they land).

Related Words

Tests requiring you to work out how two or more words are related can be quite tricky. This is because they are very much in the realm of active problem solving. They also depend much more on your understanding and ability to manipulate the meaning of words than on simple spelling or comprehension. Whether you have to fill in blanks or spot the odd one out, the process you need to go through is:

1 Establish a rule that, on the face of it, links the question words. Look at what the words are or describe them first using a simple characteristic – are they both one colour, or made of the same type of material? Be as specific as you can be.
2 Apply the rule to the target word and see if any of the answer options match the target word without breaking the rule you have applied.
3 If not, then identify where the deficit was and modify the rule.
4 Repeat the process.

For instance, which is the odd one out of the following?

Keyboard   Mouse   Telephone   Printer

We might begin by applying a rule saying, 'except for the odd one out, they are all electrical equipment'. But that doesn't work because they are all electrical. We might then say that 'they are all plastic except for the odd one out', but they all tend to be plastic so that doesn't help us. Next, we might say 'they are all used in an office except for the odd one out which is only used at home', but that doesn't give us an answer either.

You may have to work through a dozen or more rules until you find one that makes sense. In this case, the answer is that they are all computer related equipment except for the telephone.

If you suspect this is the type of test you are going to be sitting, then a useful practice technique is to find groups of three items in your own home and ask yourself, 'How are any two of these alike and different to the third?' Keep going until you have exhausted all possible traits or adjectives against which you can measure them. Begin simply with what the items do, then continue with what physical characteristics they have such as colour and size. Then move systematically into more complex characteristics such as whether they refer to specific or general concepts, and even which tense they are – future, present, or past.

Synonyms and Antonyms

The difficult part about completing tests to do with synonyms and antonyms tends not to be identifying which words mean the same as, or the opposite of, a particular word, rather understanding which of the two you are supposed to be doing. When faced with questions like 'What is the opposite of the same as …?' it is very easy to become confused. The language used is simple enough, the hard part is keeping track of it.

The best thing to do is to work through the question one step or operation at a time; often working backwards can help. So in the case of:

What is the opposite of the same as freeze?

We might say:

1 Freeze, Ok, I know what that means.
2 The same as freeze, that's just freeze again, or perhaps something like 'chill', but I know where I am with this.
3 The opposite of 'chill' or 'freeze', that would be something like 'thaw'.
4 Try not to hold the whole question in your head in one go; break it down into manageable chunks.

Problem Solving or Critical Thinking

What is being assessed here is your ability to critically evaluate information presented verbally without being swayed by irrelevant or emotive information, which may either be present in the passage, or which you yourself may bring to your interpretation of it. So, even if you know a statement to be untrue in real life you must only answer based on the information and instructions you have been given.

Watch out for statements that include qualifiers such as 'seems' or 'would appear to'. For instance, if you were presented with the statement 'Boys would seem to like playing football more than girls', it is not possible to say that this is definitely true, only that it may be.

Be aware of your own beliefs and try not to let them influence your interpretation of the facts.

4

Tests of Abstract Ability

Abstract ability refers to problem solving in a context free environment, in other words, solving problems that are not overtly numerical, verbal or mechanical in nature.

These tests are often used as a measure of high-level intellectual reasoning ability and they crop up regularly in assessments for higher-level jobs. The key ability assessed here is problem solving. You are usually presented with quite a lot of irrelevant and seemingly unrelated information. Your task is generally to separate the 'noise' from what is actually relevant to solving the problem.

Abstract Test 1 – Pattern Series

Type of test: Power

Typical length: 15–25 questions

Typical time allowed: 20–30 minutes

Used for: Intermediate / Higher level

Frequency of use: Common

In each question, your task here is to look at the upper series of four figures and work out what rule links them. Then decide which (if any) of the four following figures shares that characteristic. Give yourself 30 minutes.

1

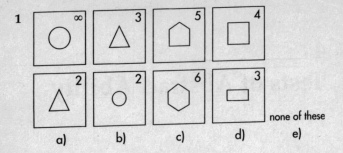

a)   b)   c)   d)   none of these   e)

2

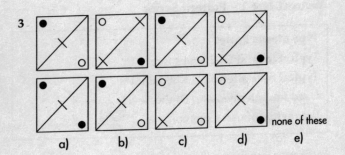

a)   b)   c)   d)   none of these   e)

3

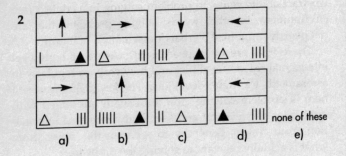

a)   b)   c)   d)   none of these   e)

4

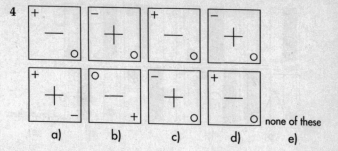

a)   b)   c)   d)   none of these

                              e)

5

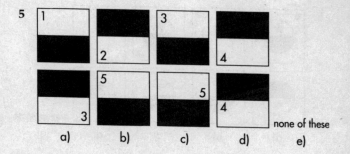

a)   b)   c)   d)   none of these

                              e)

6

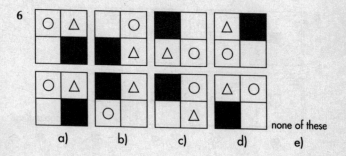

a)   b)   c)   d)   none of these

                              e)

7

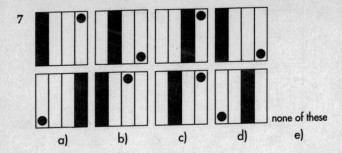

a)   b)   c)   d)   none of these
                                                               e)

8

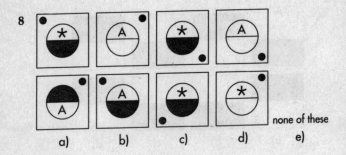

a)   b)   c)   d)   none of these
                                                               e)

9

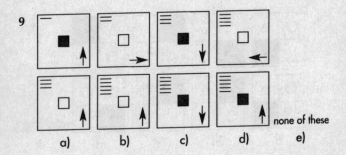

a)   b)   c)   d)   none of these
                                                               e)

10

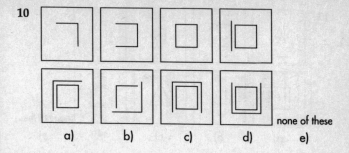

none of these

a)   b)   c)   d)   e)

11

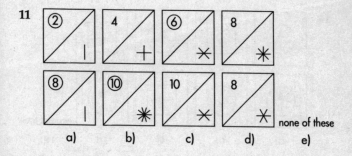

none of these

a)   b)   c)   d)   e)

12

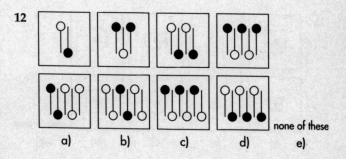

none of these

a)   b)   c)   d)   e)

13

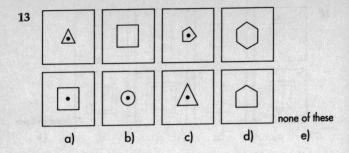

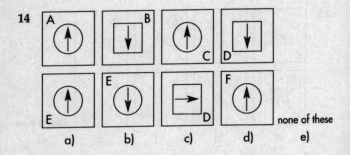

a)   b)   c)   d)   none of these

                                              e)

14

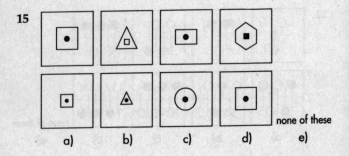

a)   b)   c)   d)   none of these

                                              e)

15

a)   b)   c)   d)   none of these

                                              e)

16

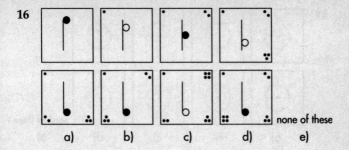

a)   b)   c)   d)   e) none of these

17

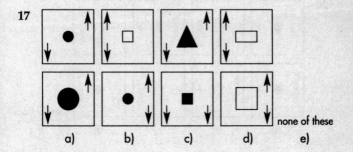

a)   b)   c)   d)   e) none of these

18

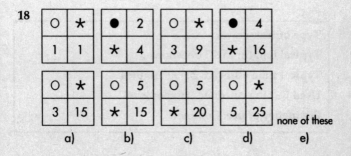

a)   b)   c)   d)   e) none of these

91

19

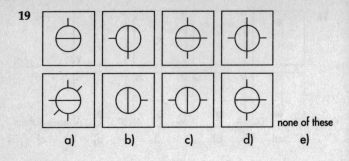

a)   b)   c)   d)   none of these
                              e)

20

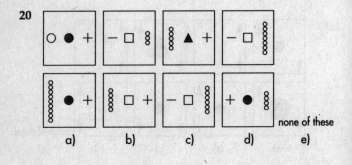

a)   b)   c)   d)   none of these
                              e)

Abstract Test 2 – Related Symbols (Odd One Out)

> **Type of test:** Power
> **Typical length:** 15–25 questions
> **Typical time allowed:** 20–30 minutes
> **Used for:** Intermediate/Higher level
> **Frequency of use:** Common

Your task here is to look at the series of five figures, work out what the rule is which links four of them and then choose which of the figures obey that rule and identify the one which does not. Give yourself 30 minutes.

1

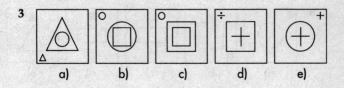

a)   b)   c)   d)   e)

2

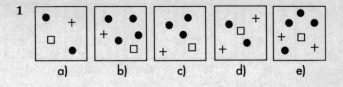

a)   b)   c)   d)   e)

3

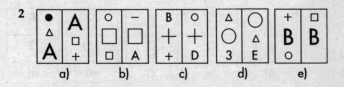

a)   b)   c)   d)   e)

4

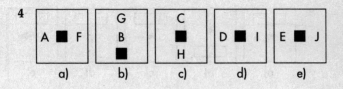

a)   b)   c)   d)   e)

5

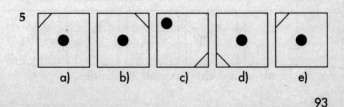

a)   b)   c)   d)   e)

6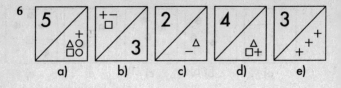

7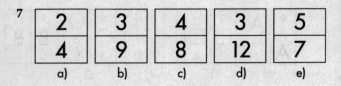

8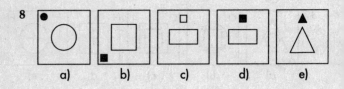

9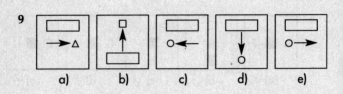

10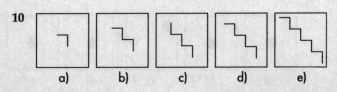

11

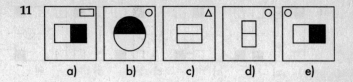

a)   b)   c)   d)   e)

12

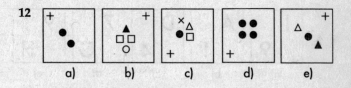

a)   b)   c)   d)   e)

13

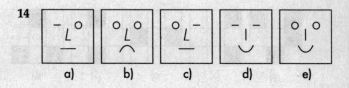

a)   b)   c)   d)   e)

14

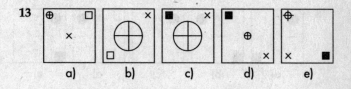

a)   b)   c)   d)   e)

15

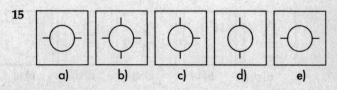

a)   b)   c)   d)   e)

16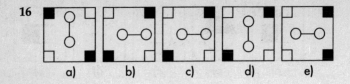

17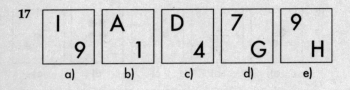

18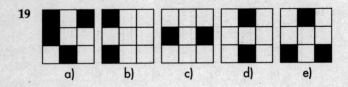

19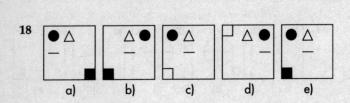

20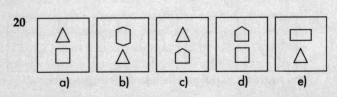

96

HINTS ON DEALING WITH ABSTRACT REASONING TESTS

- The first thing to remember is that the figures in an abstract ability test may share more than one characteristic in common, so don't just stop at the first thing in common you find.
- A simple answer may well be the correct one. Even though the question may look complex, the rule you are looking for needn't be.
- When looking for differences or commonalties in shape series, work your way systematically through all of the characteristics you can think of – shape, size, colour, location, odd and even numbers of symbols, mirror images, rotating symbols, and so on. You must be systematic and, if you are allowed, it may help to keep a running tally of the characteristics you are looking for on a piece of scrap paper and keep adding to it as you go through the test.
- Keep in mind previous rules you have found in the same test. They are likely to re-appear because the number of rules that can be applied to abstract tests is limited.
- When you think you have identified the rule that links the shapes in a series, check it by applying it to every shape with care. If even a single shape doesn't fit the rule, then the rule you have identified is wrong.
- Go through the abstract reasoning examples in this book and look for other rules that may explain the series.
- If, in an abstract series of shapes, you are given a 'none of these' answer option, don't spend too long looking for an answer that may not be there. Abstract tests are designed to confuse you with irrelevant information, so allocate yourself a set amount of time for each question and, if you cannot find the answer, move on. This is probably more efficient in the long run since it allows you move on to potentially less difficult questions.

- Sometimes, as in Abstract Test 2, the rule you are trying to find is shared by all of the shapes except the odd one out, which breaks it. However, you may also find specific questions that require you to think at the next level up. In these cases the rule is not 'all of the shapes are …', it may be something like 'if the shape has … then … else …'. In other words, two related rules may be at work. So, before you discount a rule because it only accounts for say 2 or 3 of the figures in a series, check to make the sure the other shapes are not accounted for by an inversion of the rule.

- Unless you are specifically told not to, don't forget to look for patterns or rules that relate to where a particular figure is in the series. A common form of Abstract Test 1 involves the figures sharing some rule by virtue of their place in the sequence, (for instance, figure 1 may have one small square, figure 2 may have two small squares and so on.)

5

Tests of Technical Ability

We can loosely group tests of spatial and mechanical ability together into the general category of technical ability. Tests such as these are designed to measure a person's ability to understand and apply what they know of the characteristics of the physical world to solving problems that require the manipulation of physical objects.

Mechanical reasoning ability looks specifically at how well a person can understand the basic mechanical and physical principles behind operating machinery, tools, temperature, pressure, geometry and so on.

Spatial ability is concerned with how well a person can manipulate either a two- or three- dimensional object in their head and perform some operation in the process.

Mechanical Ability Test 1

This is a very common form of a mechanical test, covering a range of mechanical or physical principles including fulcrums and levers, temperature, pressure, rotational forces and the characteristics of weights, gases and fluids.

Type of test: Speed/Power

Typical length: 25–35 questions

Typical time allowed: 20–30 minutes

Used for: Basic level

Frequency of use: Common with jobs requiring the use or understanding of mechanical devices

Read the instructions for each question and answer it as appropriate. Give yourself 25 minutes.

1 At which point will plank A be most likely to balance?

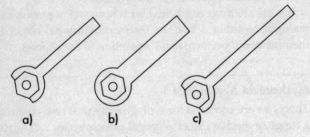

2 With which spanner will it be easiest to turn the nut?

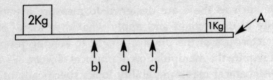

3 Which vehicle will roll fastest downhill?

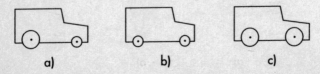

4 Which load will require the least effort to lift when rope A is pulled?

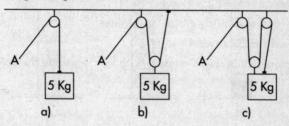

a) b) c)

5 Which tyre would sink least in soft ground?

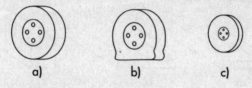

a) b) c)

6 Which screw would be easiest to tighten by hand?

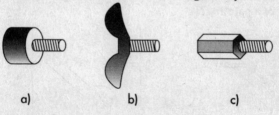

a) b) c)

7 From which container would liquid evaporate most quickly?

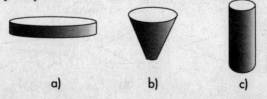

a) b) c)

8 Which tower would be most stable in strong wind?

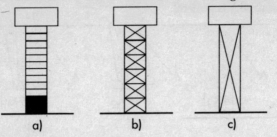

9 Through which channel would the water flow most quickly?

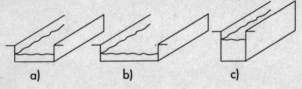

10 Which of these fixings would best support the weight of a painting?

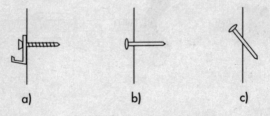

11 Which wedge will split some wood with least effort?

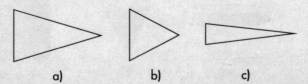

12 If switch A is closed what will happen?

a) x + y will light
b) y will light only
c) x will light only

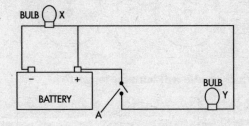

13 Which way will propeller A turn when released?

a) clockwise   b) anti-clockwise   c) neither

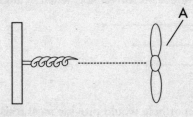

14 Which is heaviest to carry?

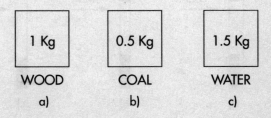

1 Kg	0.5 Kg	1.5 Kg
WOOD	COAL	WATER
a)	b)	c)

15 If wheel A turns clockwise which way will wheel B turn?

a) clockwise   b) anti-clockwise   c) neither

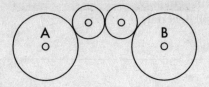

16 Which candle will burn the longest?

a)   b)   c)

17 If all 3 wires are strung to the same tension, which will produce the lowest note when strung?

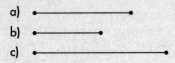

18 Which porthole would provide most resistance to the outside sea in a submarine?

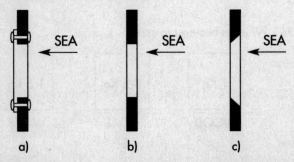

a)   b)   c)

19 If a bullet is fired from point X at a solid surface, what is its most likely trajectory after impact?

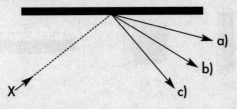

20 If lever X is lifted through 90°, in which direction will load A travel?

a) up   b) down   c) no movement   d) down then up

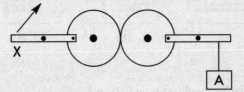

21 As the balloon rises will it:

a) increase in size
b) decrease in size
c) stay the same size

22 Which keel will provide most stability in a heavy sea?

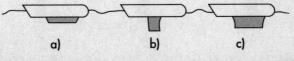

23 The pressure will be greatest at the bottom of which water filled vessel?

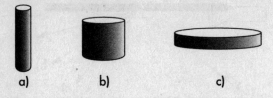

a)　　　　　　b)　　　　　　c)

24 Which cargo ship would be most stable?

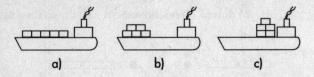

a)　　　　　　b)　　　　　　c)

25 Which wheelbarrow will be easiest to lift?

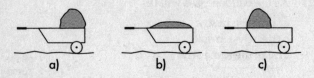

a)　　　　　　b)　　　　　　c)

26 Where will the moon appear lowest on the horizon?

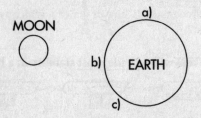

27 Which torch will throw the sharpest beam?

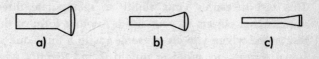

28 Which nail will be the easiest to drive into a piece of wood?

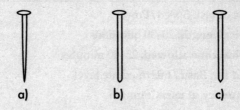

29 Which container will have most water displaced from it when object A is dropped into it?

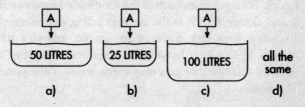

30 Each pan contains 1 litre of water – which will evaporate first?

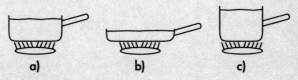

Spatial Test 1 – Constructing Objects

This test measures your ability to manipulate three-dimensional objects in your head. Another form of this test is one where you are presented with a three-dimensional figure and asked to unfold it and identify what the unfolded shape would look like. The principles of, and operations carried out, in both types of test are the same.

Type of test: Speed/Power

Typical length: 20–30 questions

Typical time allowed: 25–40 minutes

Used for: Basic/Intermediate level

Frequency of use: Common

For every question, your task is to examine the unfolded figure. Then consider each of the four folded figures below it and decide which is the corresponding folded version. To make your task easier there are no 'none of these' options in this test, however it does occur in other versions of this test that you may come across. Give yourself 30 minutes.

1

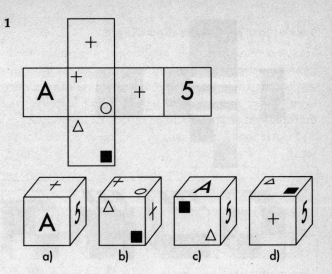

2

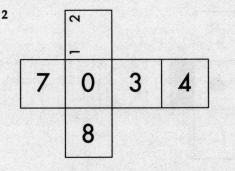

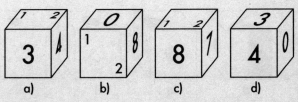

3

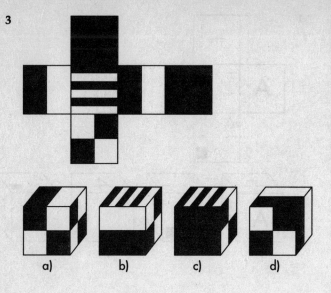

a) b) c) d)

4

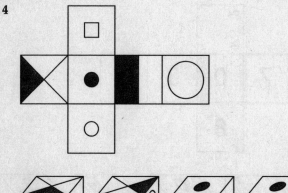

a) b) c) d)

5

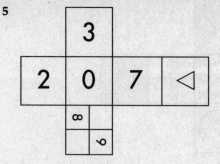

a)   b)   c)   d)

6

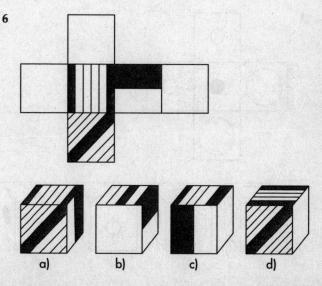

a)   b)   c)   d)

7

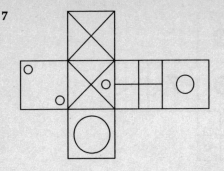

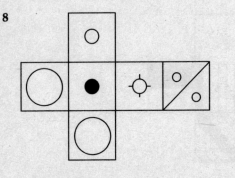

a)   b)   c)   d)

8

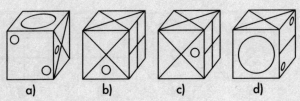

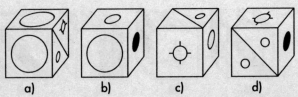

a)   b)   c)   d)

112

9

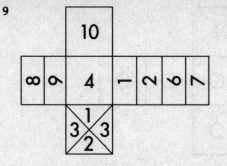

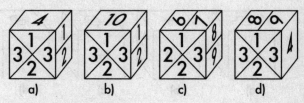

10

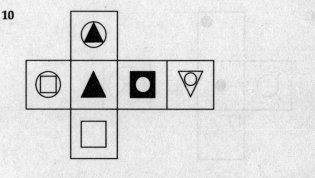

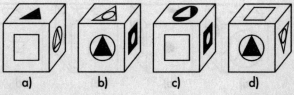

11

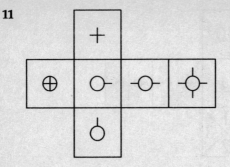

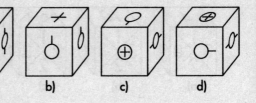

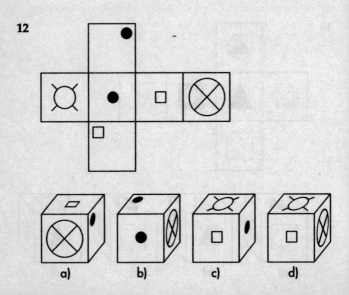

13

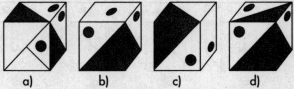

14

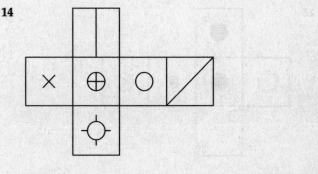

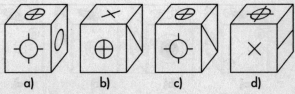

15

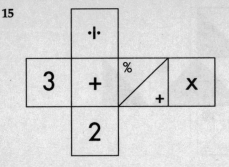

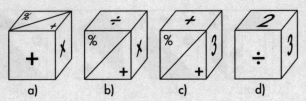

16

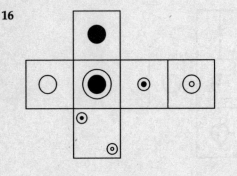

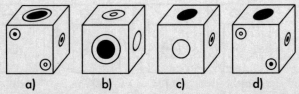

17

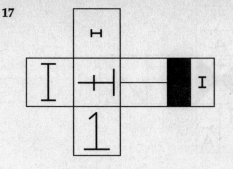

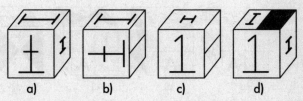

18

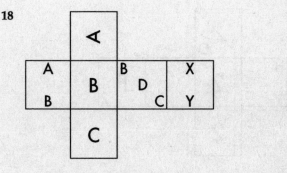

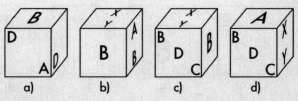

19

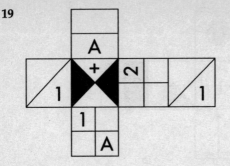

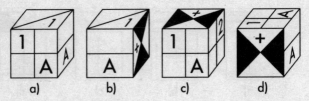

20

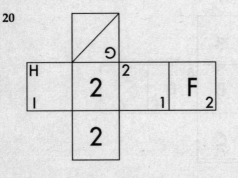

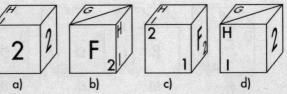

21

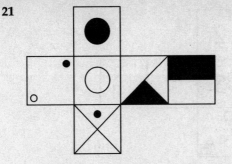

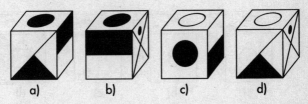

a)   b)   c)   d)

22

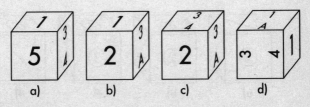

a)   b)   c)   d)

23

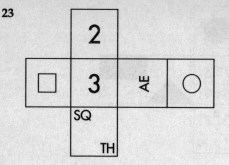

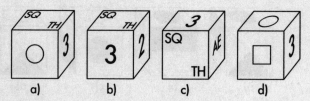

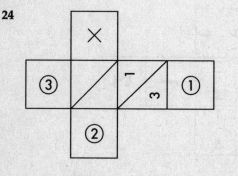

24

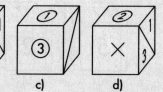

25

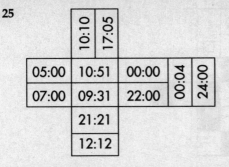

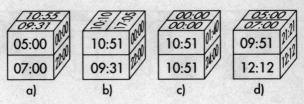

a) b) c) d)

26

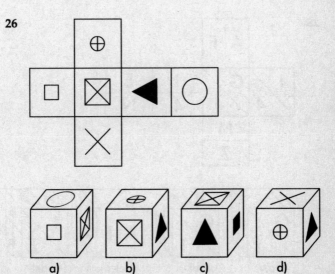

a) b) c) d)

27

28

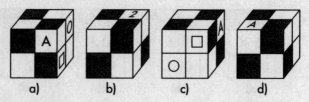

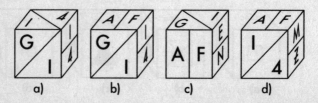

29

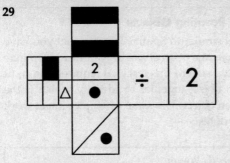

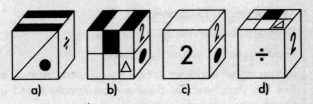

30

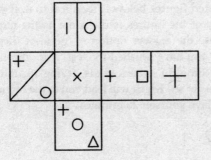

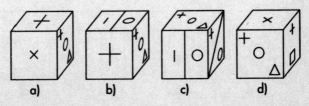

Spatial Test 2 – Rotating Objects

This is somewhat similar to Spatial Test 1 in that you have to manipulate an image of an object in your head. You may sometimes see a version of this test that requires you to fit two halves of an object together or identify which is the mirror image of an object. The same principles are at work in all three types of test.

Type of test: Speed/Power

Typical length: 15–25 questions

Typical time allowed: 20–30 minutes

Used for: Basic/Intermediate level

Frequency of use: Rare to find a dedicated test such as this but items such as these are commonly found in broader measures of spatial ability

---

Your task here is to look at the target figure and decide which of the rotated figures below is identical to it. If you do not think any of the figures is the same as the target shape then choose the answer option e) 'none of these'. A day or so after you have finished the test, work through it again but this time do it backwards, trying to unfold each of the answers to see which will lead you to the original question figure. Give yourself 25 minutes.

1

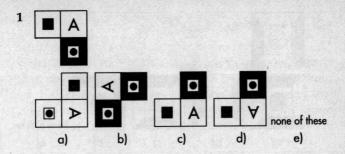

none of these

a)   b)   c)   d)   e)

2

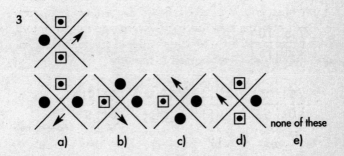

none of these

a)   b)   c)   d)   e)

3

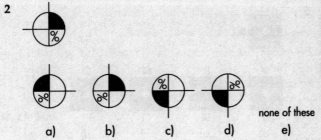

none of these

a)   b)   c)   d)   e)

4

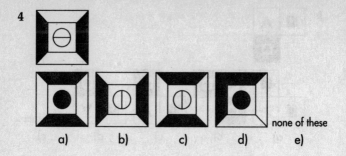

a)   b)   c)   d)   none of these

                                                        e)

5

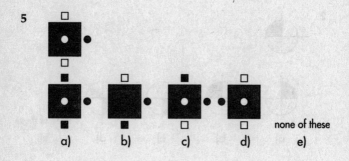

a)   b)   c)   d)   none of these

                                                        e)

6

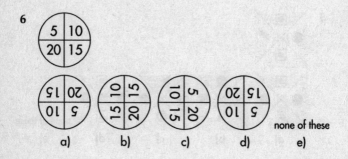

a)   b)   c)   d)   none of these

                                                        e)

7

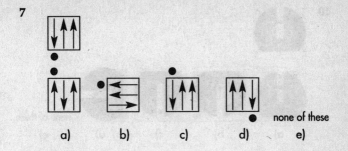

a)   b)   c)   d)   e) none of these

8

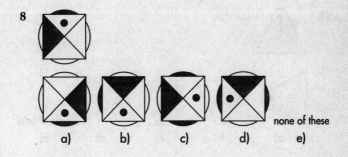

a)   b)   c)   d)   e) none of these

9

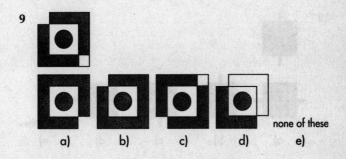

a)   b)   c)   d)   e) none of these

10

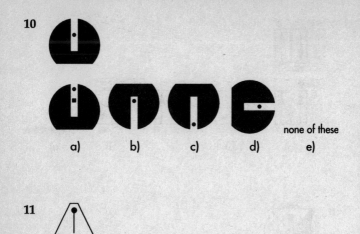

a)   b)   c)   d)   none of these
e)

11

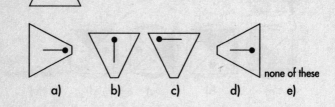

a)   b)   c)   d)   none of these
e)

12

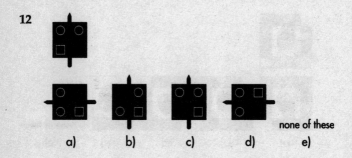

a)   b)   c)   d)   none of these
e)

128

13

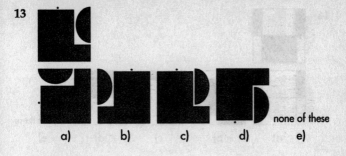

a)   b)   c)   d)   none of these   e)

14

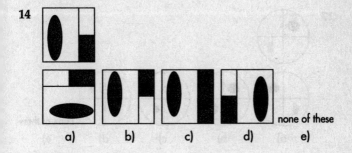

a)   b)   c)   d)   none of these   e)

15

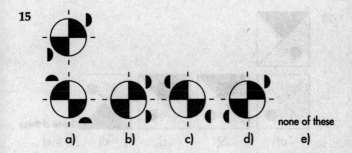

a)   b)   c)   d)   none of these   e)

16

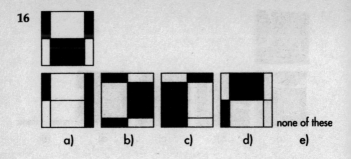

a)　　b)　　c)　　d)　　none of these
　　　　　　　　　　　　　　　　e)

17

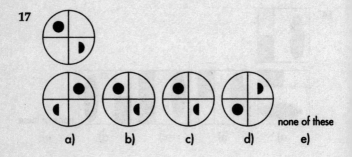

a)　　b)　　c)　　d)　　none of these
　　　　　　　　　　　　　　　　e)

18

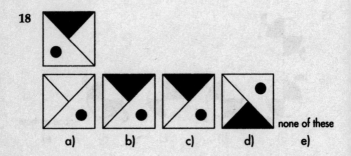

a)　　b)　　c)　　d)　　none of these
　　　　　　　　　　　　　　　　e)

130

19

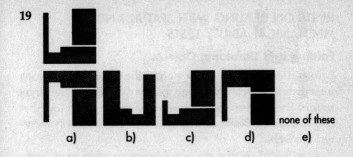

a)   b)   c)   d)   e) none of these

20

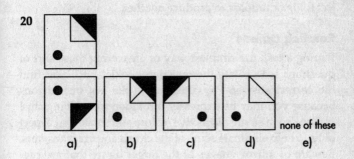

a)   b)   c)   d)   e) none of these

HINTS ON DEALING WITH SPATIAL AND MECHANICAL ABILITY TESTS

Folding and Unfolding Objects

Before attempting to fold or unfold the object, try and look for a distinctive feature on only one or two sides of the target figure. Then picture how those two sides might fit together and use this to eliminate one or two of the obviously incorrect answers.

Practise by cutting up cereal boxes or other containers. This is an excellent way of seeing in real space how an object folds or unfolds to produce another.

Rotating Objects

During a test, the simplest way of answering these sort of questions is to rotate the question booklet until you find the correct answer. Pay attention to the test instructions because you may be expressly forbidden from doing this!

Look for a single distinctive feature and rotate that aspect only, to help eliminate some of the clearly incorrect answers. Beware of mirror images of the target figure that are presented to you upside down. These can look very similar to the target figure.

Carefully check your chosen answer as there may be some small feature such as a reversed symbol or unshaded shape that you have overlooked. Paying attention to detail is the key here.

Mechanical Reasoning

There is no simple way of preparing yourself for this type of test since the type of questions asked can vary so much. The best way of approaching it is to visualize the object in question and try to see in your mind's eye how it would react when the given operation is carried out upon it. The examples given here are pretty representative and should give you a good idea of what to expect.

6

Tests of Speed and Perception

Tests of speed and perception tend to be used with candidates who are applying for jobs that will require the job holder to deal with detailed information. They tend to be used for clerical and administrative jobs, especially where the checking or processing of large amounts of data is required.

The emphasis with tests of this type is on how quickly a person can carry out the task with a minimum of error. There is almost no reasoning ability required, so while some of the tests may look like verbal or numerical tests, no actual problem solving is expected. These tests are as close as you will get to an outright speed test, and they can be used at all levels.

In one sense, all psychometric tests are tests of speed and perception as they require the test taker to take in and use information in order to solve a problem. It follows that since all such tests tend to be timed, they all have an aspect of speed and accuracy of perception.

Speed and Perception Test 1 – Checking Information

This type of test is a general measure of speed and perceptual ability. It is context free in that the information you deal with has no particular meaning – it is a very pure measure of this ability. Although it may seem as though there are a lot of questions to answer in a very short space of time, you will find that once you get going you will really move quickly. Because of this, the example questions you get at the start of a test such as this may be quite extensive, not only to show you how to make your responses, but also to bring you up to your maximum speed.

Type of test: Speed

Typical length: 40–60 questions

Typical time allowed: 10–15 minutes

Used for: All levels

Frequency of use: Less common

Your task here is to read the information in column 1, then check to see if column 2 tallies with it. If you find an error then you should circle it. Give yourself 15 minutes.

	Column 1	Column 2
1	MæYy6++aT†š&	MæYY6++aT†š&
2	XnP¢Ÿþl′1‴X	XnP¢Ÿþ**1‴X
3	þ(¹‚Ö⎮=ãaf?a	þ(¹‚Ö⎮=ãaf?a
4	hÚý>aÔmgŸDÓ	hÚý>aÔmHŸDÓ
5	ÌVÅÊa❑%″ÜÊ$′	ÌVÅÊa❑%″ÜÊ$′
6	″ª(;a®X˜˜»ýª	″ª(;a®X˜˜»ýª
7	Š‚Ö·OëOò&To×	Š‚Ö·OYTò&To×
8	ú×üÎ2ûMÓ¢ø¥á	ú×üÎ2ûMÓ¢ø¥á
9	″°µ❑+aSûa,*a	″°µ❑/*Sûa,*a
10	ÛaXÆ<±❑″aÌ¹⁄4c	ÛaXÆ<±❑″;′¹⁄4c
11	å$t5ËëÑê1ßêí	å$t5ËëÑê1ßêí
12	auke§i~3❑æéî	Auke$″~3❑æéî
13	–š{KX[KŠS$❑«	–š{KX[KŠS$❑«
14	⎮P]J³aaarflm	⎮P]J³Aearflm

#		
15	f⁻[¢|5mýy•*I	f⁻[¢|5mýy•*I
16	ÿ ^G']A¨ë>aø	ÿ ^G']A¨ë>aø
17	❑❑iªZø…u=·"G	❑❑iªZø….=·"G
18	Óśa[›…,u&/ßJ	Óśa[›…,u&/ßJ
19	g"†Š6uã÷q,ÈÊ	g"†Š6uã÷q,EÊ
20	❑-gsoyiåœñ\[	❑-gsoyiåœñ\[
21	OaÉaÑ8t'aeYX	OaÉaÑ8t'aeYX
22	pAaaGZ–Š™Ï~p	PAaaGZ+Š™Ï~p
23	‡)à³⁄₄aÂ∂·@aañ	‡)à³⁄₄aÂ∂·@aañ
24	/öŸ‹âÒm%²Òaˆ	/öŸ‹âÒm£$Òaˆ
25	%¹⁄₄W¹⁄₂HÑÒ&³iYa	%¹⁄₄W¹⁄₂HÑÒ&³iYa
26	aŠ7a‹å(.a"❑×	aŠ7a‹å(.a"❑×
27	³×¹⁄₄Sý™â❑^Ïþa	³×¹⁄₄Sý™â❑^Ïþa
28	❑ax?dñ❑°Å®éµ	❑aX?dñ❑°Å®éµ
29	aÁaûH?h‡)ÿ,G	aÁaûH?h‡)ÿ,G
30	Ìanãjú=a✧«&î	Ìanãjú=a✧«&î
31	×õ÷aa.*Éÿayã	×õ÷aa.*Éÿayã
32	^a³⁄₄³Đ<3á«µñ❑	^a³⁄₄³Đ<3á«µñ❑
33	fá-FaØi÷'ë¶¥	fá-ftØi÷'ë¶¥
34	£fµa)❑3çBa±È	£fµa)❑3çBa±È
35	ó,©;aüV¥Ô5a;	ó,©;aüV¥Ô5a;
36	VÒµé⁻4aaéˣ>a	VÒµé⁻4eeéˣ>a
37	²†OajÅ✧†OmÒ<	²†OajÅ✧†OmÒ<
38	Ö±°ša…Â›pT❑d	Ö±°ša…Â›pT❑d
39	a.aî[o-ÑC-w{	a.aî[o-ÑC-w{
40	❑ap*6V¿õ÷❑]ᵢ	❑ap*6V¿õ*/]ᵢ
41	Çÿ aâxWRña×Ù	Çÿ aâxWRña×Ù
42	ôKH5?ô‹Ëo±ÛÚ	ôKH5?ô‹Ëo±ÛÚ
43	M5Äf×÷Lïoday	M5Äf×÷Lïoday

44	ÑG¼,ŠÂ#±ŸË;?	ÑG¼,ŠÂ#±ŸË;?
45	§ÒîõaaÝèËaØg	§ÒîõaaÝeËaØg
46	ña›aÅaÄ″µ❏¡I	ña›aÅaÄ″µ❏¡I
47	a❏¸;apã!÷na†	a❏¸;apã!÷na†
48	a÷aT°—Oúër£K	a÷e4°—Oúër£K
49	•⁻ë¥❏aSÿ ′±á	•⁻ë¥❏aSÿ ′±á
50	ÿûajŸú?O®GÄ7	ŸûajŸú<O®GÄ7
51	a°o‹lQa©⁻øoN	a°o‹lQa©⁻øoN
52	¶Õ✧‰‚íu}aKÙu	¶Õ✧‰‚íu}aKÙu
53	aamaaaÛ:y£Í3	AaamaaÛ:y£Í3
54	❏³ª³a″¶?|»¹⁄₂Z	❏³ª³a″¶?|»¹⁄₂Z
55	Š#S—úó‚JŸ7aê	Š#S—úo‚JŸ7aê
56	Ö<°Y❏áaþÊš÷Ç	Ö<°Y❏áaþÊš÷Ç
57	Z^‡¬Í¡YYΦÉâk	Z^‡¬Í¡YYYÉâk
58	mÿjò<Âaa\¢™C	mÿjò<Âaa\¢™C
59	K/˜a′ãtgaÏ©£	K/˜a′ãtgaÏ©£
60	Ë¿ÄΦa¾″HþÂSã	Ë¿ÄPa¾″HþÂSã

Speed and Perception Test 2 – Checking Information

This is similar to Test 1, but you are now introduced to some meaningful information. The challenge for you here is to stop reading the information in chunks and go down to the specific letter level of detail.

You will remember from the verbal reasoning tests that we tend to read blocks of letters and 'see' whole words rather than read individual letters. You must avoid this temptation. At first glance you may not find any errors, but go beyond the meaning of what you see and just look at the raw textual information a letter at a time.

Type of test: Speed

Typical length: 20–40 questions

Typical time allowed: 20–25 minutes

Used for: All levels

Frequency of use: Common

As with Test 1 your task here is to read the information in column one, compare it with the information in column two and circle any errors you may find. There may be more than one error in each case so work carefully. Give yourself 25 minutes.

	Column 1	Column 2
1	Mr P S Bowman 76 Agriola St Acton London Order ref: 57945A	Mr P S Bowman 76 Agricola St Acton London Order ref: 57945A
2	Ms C A Howey 98 Sunderland Road Esprick Surrey Order ref: 134922B	Ms C A Howey 98 Sunderland Road Esprisk Surrey Order ref: 13922B
3	Ms C D West 24 Clifton Avenue East Creech Northants Order ref: 4457Z	Ms C D West 24 Clifton Avenue East Creach Northhants Order ref: 4457Z
4	Mrs J Chapmund 1 Coatsworth Road Fulsworth Manchester Order ref: 55741Z	Ms J Chapmund 1 Coatsworth Road Fulworth Manchester Order ref: 554171Z

5	Mr ER Hardy	Mr ER Hardy
	Salisbury House	Sailisbury House
	Kentbridge Walk	Kentsbridge Walk
	Galsworthy	Galsworthy
	East Sussex	East Sussex
	Order ref: 9754112A	Order ref: 975412A
6	Mrs B Ledon	Mrs B Ledon
	11a Cambridge Ave	11a Cambridge Ave
	Matland	Maitland
	Avon	Avon
	Order ref: 32145A	Order ref: 31245A
7	Ms Madine	Mrs Madine
	12b Bexhill Rd	12b Bexhill Rd
	Musbury	Muxbury
	Lancashire	Lancashire
	Order ref: 2251A	Order ref: 21251A
8	Mr S Patterson	Mr S Patterson
	3 Leyburn Place	3 Layburn Place
	Polbay	Polbay
	Swansea	Swansea
	Wales	Wales
	Order ref: 122313F	Order ref: 122313F
9	Mr Oulsby	Mr Olsby
	25 Ripon St	25 Ripon St
	Sourin	Sourin
	Isle of Wight	Isle of Wight
	Order ref: 1521114A	Order ref: 152114A
10	Mrs LK Brown	Ms LK Brown
	6 Kellis lane	6 Kelis lane
	Boughwood	Boughwood
	West Yorkshire	West Yorkshire
	Order ref: 225287B	Order ref: 225287B

11	Mr Askew	Mr Askew
	2c March Court	2c March Court
	Bodney	Bodney
	Devon	Devon
	Order ref: 1534B	Order ref: 1534B

12	Mr Mulgrew	Mr Mulgrew
	33 Elm Road	33 Elm Road
	Ganarew	Glanarew
	Argyll	Argyll
	Order ref: 176585A	Order ref: 176855A

13	Mrs S Riley	Mr S Riley
	227b Milling Road	272b Milling Road
	Foulsham	Foulsham
	Chelsea	Chelsea
	London	London
	Order ref: 485799Z	Order ref: 485799A

14	Ms AM Wann	Ms AW Mann
	12 Brecon Place	12 Brecon Place
	Gaer	Gaer
	Isle of Skye	Ilse of Skye
	Order ref: 196536Z	Order ref: 196536Z

15	Ms L Marshall	Ms L Marshall
	62 Portmead Rise	62 Portmead Rise
	Lindsell	Lindsell
	Co Durham	Co Durham
	Order ref: 795455A	Order ref: 795455A

16	Ms Bennet	Ms J Bennet
	Palace House	Palace House
	Westover Place	Westover Place
	Kensington	Kensington
	London	London
	Order ref: 98561A	Order ref: 98561A

17	Mrs R Clark	Ms R Clark
	121 North Dene Court	121 North Dene Court
	Letterbreane	Letterbeane
	Somerset	Somerset
	Order ref: 87978B	Order ref: 87978B

18 Mr A Chishack   Mr A Chishack
8a Lyne Lane   8a Lyne Lane
Ridely   Ridely
Northumberland   Northumberland
Order ref: 4871FF   Order ref: 4871FF

19 Ms D Gulbrand   Ms D Guldbran
1 Mann Court   1 Man Court
Purslowe   Purslowe
Cornwall   Cornwall
Order ref: 2298147F   Order ref: 2298147F

20 Mr A Docherty   Mr AB Docherty
1 The Larches   1 The Larches
Rhoslan Place   Rhoslan Place
Rimpton   Rimpton
Lancaster   Lancaster
Order ref: 458721B   Order ref: 458712B

21 Mr GD West   Mr GD West
23 Meadow Lane   23 Meadow Lane
Sutton Cross   Sutton Cross
Willand   Willand
Buckinghamshire   Buckinghamshire
Order ref: 33658B   Order ref: 33658B

22 Mr Dixon   Mr Dixon
86 Farlisle Place   86 Fairlisle Place
Whincle   Whincle
Aylesbury   Aylesbury
Order ref: 45687A   Order ref: 45687A

23   Mrs JK Charlton   Mrs JK Charlton
       Plaid House   Pliad House
       Kingsway   Kingsway
       Achfary   Achfary
       West Lothian   Wets Lothian
       Order ref: 24555Z   Order ref: 24555Z

24   Ms JL Somers   Ms JL Sommers
       55b Runnymeade Road 55b Runnymeade Road
       Wimslow   Wilmslow
       Order ref: 44887A   Order ref: 44887A

25   Mr Toogood   Mr Togood
       101 Thorntree Walk   101 Thorntree Walk
       Burholme Rise   Burholme Rise
       Etal   Etals
       Hampshire   Hampshire
       Order ref: 1165B   Order ref: 1165B

26   Mrs Leithead   Mrs Lethead
       114 Athrington Court   114 Athrington Court
       Helington   Hellington
       Inverness   Inverness
       Order ref: 11654B   Order ref: 11654B

27   Mr F Francotte   Mr F Francote
       77 Fieldside   77 Fieldside
       Longthorpe   Longthorpe
       Cambridgeshire   Cambridgeshire
       Order ref: 1158964Z   Order ref: 158964Z

28   Ms B Mossam   Ms B Mossam
       34 Myrtle Street   34 Mirtle Street
       Stichill Town   Stickill Town
       Glasgow   Glasgow
       Order ref: 19678Z   Order ref: 19678Z

29	Mr Saenger	Mr Seanger
	1 Huntcliffe Gardens	1 Huntcliffe Gardens
	Pentire Way	Penlire Way
	Wilburton	Wilburton
	Leeds	Leeds
	Order ref: 4567A	Order ref: 4567A
30	Mr MN McDonald	Mr M MacDonald
	11a Bruce Close	11a Bruce Close
	Bretby	Bretsby
	Edinburgh	Edinburgh
	Order ref: 555887B	Order ref: 555887B

Speed and Perception Test 3 – Copying Information

Unlike the two tests you have done so far, this next one requires you to copy information rather than just compare it. Like Test 1, this test presents you with a context-free set of information – information that has no inherent meaning. This is because otherwise you would rely on your spelling and word comprehension ability and this would defeat the point of assessing accuracy of perception. You will need to score this test yourself.

Different versions of this test may ask you to put letters and numbers in specific order. As an extra practice, when you have finished this test go through it two more times:

1 Copying the information across in numerical and alphabetical order, with numbers coming before letters, and lowercase letters coming before uppercase letters.
2 Copying the information across in reverse order.

Type of test:	Speed	
Typical length:	20–40 questions	
Typical time allowed:	10–20 minutes	
Used for:	All levels	
Frequency of use:	Common	

Your task here is to copy the information in column 1 across to column 2. Give yourself 15 minutes.

1	AaD12GgrRHtt	_ _ _ _ _ _ _ _ _ _ _ _
2	dDFG6e7RTtrrs	_ _ _ _ _ _ _ _ _ _ _ _
3	Nnft3OOghhii	_ _ _ _ _ _ _ _ _ _ _ _
4	SsjjtfoOSWwe	_ _ _ _ _ _ _ _ _ _ _ _
5	cCJJ5Mm6paaa	_ _ _ _ _ _ _ _ _ _ _ _
6	aaLLLEd4n4tt	_ _ _ _ _ _ _ _ _ _ _ _
7	SSSl2qq1qtts	_ _ _ _ _ _ _ _ _ _ _ _
8	iiiOOllfsfsf	_ _ _ _ _ _ _ _ _ _ _ _
9	jjjllssSTT2e	_ _ _ _ _ _ _ _ _ _ _ _
10	PPPL0kkOWwqq	_ _ _ _ _ _ _ _ _ _ _ _
11	cCZZSDxTXtxt	_ _ _ _ _ _ _ _ _ _ _ _
12	dDLLPtp6UYuy	_ _ _ _ _ _ _ _ _ _ _ _
13	qQQnnfsDsttt	_ _ _ _ _ _ _ _ _ _ _ _
14	ssDD8loIOitt	_ _ _ _ _ _ _ _ _ _ _ _
15	pPLI8NIonINi	_ _ _ _ _ _ _ _ _ _ _ _
16	wwLWl7lttht	_ _ _ _ _ _ _ _ _ _ _ _
17	dfDFDfdfDfgh	_ _ _ _ _ _ _ _ _ _ _ _
18	njWWittPLlcc	_ _ _ _ _ _ _ _ _ _ _ _
19	s5skjk5TTtpAa	_ _ _ _ _ _ _ _ _ _ _ _
20	tFTFg4gtgTHh	_ _ _ _ _ _ _ _ _ _ _ _

21	sDSD3esES3Se	_ _ _ _ _ _ _ _ _ _ _
22	PTP7ptTTP7py	_ _ _ _ _ _ _ _ _ _ _
23	LLLKkjtUTUtu	_ _ _ _ _ _ _ _ _ _ _
24	SSdd2DEdfrfr	_ _ _ _ _ _ _ _ _ _ _
25	sSsnNN22titi	_ _ _ _ _ _ _ _ _ _ _
26	aaAIIeiwwEWe	_ _ _ _ _ _ _ _ _ _ _
27	kKT1FofoTINI	_ _ _ _ _ _ _ _ _ _ _
28	dD11lllYYYy	_ _ _ _ _ _ _ _ _ _ _
29	DD2dllLLWwqq	_ _ _ _ _ _ _ _ _ _ _
30	BDB88dBBddbd	_ _ _ _ _ _ _ _ _ _ _
31	ITTtiTITittt	_ _ _ _ _ _ _ _ _ _ _
32	jljLljjr5JLj	_ _ _ _ _ _ _ _ _ _ _
33	sSSs4TTTsttt	_ _ _ _ _ _ _ _ _ _ _
34	opOOpopqpQPQ	_ _ _ _ _ _ _ _ _ _ _
35	PQPQ3qPPQqqq	_ _ _ _ _ _ _ _ _ _ _
36	ddDKdkdKSSs	_ _ _ _ _ _ _ _ _ _ _
37	eeEJ6jejfFgf	_ _ _ _ _ _ _ _ _ _ _
38	WWwvwYWVvyw	_ _ _ _ _ _ _ _ _ _ _
39	nMNNmnmNNNmn	_ _ _ _ _ _ _ _ _ _ _
40	aeEE4eaeaa4A	_ _ _ _ _ _ _ _ _ _ _

HINTS ON DEALING WITH TESTS OF SPEED AND PERCEPTION

- The key to dealing with these types of test is to work at a level of fine detail. Do not be fooled into thinking that a quick glance will help you find an error – it may with the more obvious ones, but you will miss things like subtle letter changes. So work your way through each question a letter at a time.

- More than with any other type of test, you will need to concentrate. If you take a breather, even for a minute, you will lose the speed and momentum you have built up.
- This type of test tends to be shorter in terms of time than other types – work as quickly as you can and keep up the pace.
- When you have finished, or are coming to the last few minutes of the test, go through and check your answers. You will have increased your familiarity with the items and might spot a mistake you have previously missed the second time round.

7
Personality Tests

The most common type of psychometric test you may come across is a personality test. In fact, to call a personality test a 'test' is not strictly accurate since the results of personality tests are descriptive or narrative in nature. Most personality tests view personality as being made up of a series of traits. At either extreme of these traits, you will find a description of a behaviour such as assertive or submissive.

Personality test questions come in two general forms. The first asks you to comment on which descriptive terms or action, are most like you or most likely to describe what you would do in a given situation. For example:

Which is most like you?

a) Loud
b) Rule conscious

The second form of question presents the information the other way around. For example:

'I am a loud person.'

a) agree
b) disagree

The first type of question makes a direct comparison between two traits, and is used to produce a report or profile that may say:

'This person is more loud than rule conscious.'

This removes the need for a comparison group against which to compare a person's score. Naturally, tests like this cannot be used in a situation such as selection or recruitment where people are being compared, because all they say is that you are more one thing than you are another, not how much of one thing you actually are.

The second type of question only asks about a single trait, and the score obtained can be used to make comparisons between people using a norm group.

Personality tests are very flexible and they are frequently used since they measure general traits that can be linked up with a great many specific jobs. For instance, a trait such as assertiveness could be relevant in sales, law enforcement, and customer services. Also, different traits can be combined to produce a richer picture of the individual taking the test.

Try the personality test below. It is based on a real personality test although it has been slightly changed from its original form. However, it should still give you a pretty good indication of your own personality.

Because personality tests are descriptive, and trait descriptions are interpreted in a way that involves asking 'Is this trait relevant to this particular job?' there are no right or wrong answers. Use the scoring key at the end of the test to calculate your own scores.

Personality Test

This questionnaire is designed to investigate the characteristics possessed by different people. It asks about various subjects such as attitudes to other people, the things an individual likes doing and how they would feel or behave in certain situations. The general format of the questions is:

1 I find people with different views to my own interesting

    a) agree b) disagree

When answering the questions, bear the following in mind:

- There are no 'right' or 'wrong' answers.
- Do not spend more than a few seconds thinking about the answer to any one question. It is best to give the first answer that occurs to you.
- Answer all of the questions.
- Be honest and give answers that you feel describe you best.
- If you are stuck on a question, then mark the answer that would best describe how you would behave in general.

1 I will happily wait for something if I have to.

    a) agree b) disagree   ___

2 I really get upset when things are going wrong.

    a) agree b) disagree   ___

3 I do not get annoyed very easily.

    a) agree b) disagree   ___

4 I am a calm person.

    a) agree b) disagree   ___

5 Sometimes I get really frustrated with things.

    a) agree b) disagree   ___

6 I don't mind other people giving me orders.

    a) agree b) disagree   ___

7 I am happy enough to criticize others.

a) agree   b) disagree   _____

8 I don't mind others not doing what I say.

a) agree   b) disagree   _____

9 I would rather give in than get my own way through aggression.

a) agree   b) disagree   _____

10 I prefer to compromise than fight with someone.

a) agree   b) disagree   _____

11 I would prefer a job that was predictable to one which was unpredictable.

a) agree   b) disagree   _____

12 Other people think I am a careful person.

a) agree   b) disagree   _____

13 I prefer people making informed decisions to taking a chance.

a) agree   b) disagree   _____

14 It is not worth risking things to gain an advantage.

a) agree   b) disagree   _____

15 I do things spontaneously.

a) agree   b) disagree   _____

16 I can find rules too restrictive.

a) agree   b) disagree   _____

17 I would like to be seen as someone who breaks the rules for a higher cause.

a) agree b) disagree ___

18 I do not like rules laid down by others.

a) agree b) disagree ___

19 If I think a rule is unnecessary I will not follow it.

a) agree b) disagree ___

20 If you can break the rules and get away with it then do so.

a) agree b) disagree ___

21 I don't like being the centre of attention.

a) agree b) disagree ___

22 I am uncomfortable speaking up in a group.

a) agree b) disagree ___

23 Meeting new people makes me nervous.

a) agree b) disagree ___

24 I get nervous about doing presentations or speeches.

a) agree b) disagree ___

25 In a group I would rather listen to other people than talk myself.

a) agree b) disagree ___

26 I am quite a logical person.

a) agree b) disagree ___

27 I prefer an action or adventure film to a romantic drama.

a) agree   b) disagree   ____

28 Technical skills are worth more than artistic talent.

a) agree   b) disagree   ____

29 Being sensitive to others is a good thing.

a) agree   b) disagree   ____

30 I don't take criticism personally.

a) agree   b) disagree   ____

31 I don't waste time worrying about whether or not I can trust someone.

a) agree   b) disagree   ____

32 Even when I may have been taken advantage of, I still view people positively.

a) agree   b) disagree   ____

33 I trust the people I meet.

a) agree   b) disagree   ____

34 People usually mean well.

a) agree   b) disagree   ____

35 I am careful of other people's intentions.

a) agree   b) disagree   ____

36 I am happier dealing with practical details than theories and strategies.

a) agree   b) disagree   ____

37 I prefer facts to possibilities.

a) agree   b) disagree   ___

38 I am a 'hands on' person.

a) agree   b) disagree   ___

39 I can get wrapped up in my own thoughts.

a) agree   b) disagree   ___

40 I am more imaginative than practical.

a) agree   b) disagree   ___

41 I wish people would deal with logic more than emotion.

a) agree   b) disagree   ___

42 I tend not to discuss my feelings with other people.

a) agree   b) disagree   ___

43 I keep myself to myself.

a) agree   b) disagree   ___

44 I am a private person.

a) agree   b) disagree   ___

45 I am cautious about getting too involved with people.

a) agree   b) disagree   ___

46 At times I take on too much and worry that I can't cope.

a) agree   b) disagree   ___

47 Sometime I feel frightened for no logical reason.

a) agree   b) disagree   ___

48 You have to do things to make people like you.

a) agree   b) disagree   ___

49 I get in a bad mood when running out of time on a task.

a) agree   b) disagree   ___

50 I worry other people will not approve of me.

a) agree   b) disagree   ___

51 Most risks are unnecessary.

a) agree   b) disagree   ___

52 I view a change in job with some anxiety.

a) agree   b) disagree   ___

53 Most change is made for no good reason.

a) agree   b) disagree   ___

54 I prefer existing stability to not knowing what will happen.

a) agree   b) disagree   ___

55 I would like a job that was different but had little security.

a) agree   b) disagree   ___

56 I do not like working alone.

a) agree   b) disagree   ___

57 I perform better on a project when others are involved.

a) agree   b) disagree   ___

58 I feel lonely if I have no contact with other people.

a) agree   b) disagree   _____

59 I enjoy the company of others.

a) agree   b) disagree   _____

60 I prefer to work without distractions from others.

a) agree   b) disagree   _____

HOW TO SCORE THE PERSONALITY TEST

1 Score 0 points for 'agree' and 1 for 'disagree', except for questions 4, 5, 15, 39, 40 and 55 which are scored 1 point for 'agree' and 0 points for 'disagree'.

2 Add together your scores using the following table.

Trait	Add scores from question numbers	Total
Emotionality	1–5	
Assertiveness	6–10	
Enthusiasm	11–15	
Social Confidence	16–20	
Rule Orientation	21–25	
Sensitivity	26–30	
Caution	31–35	
Cognitive style	36–40	
Openness	41–45	
Self-Esteem	46–50	
Adaptability	51–55	
Independence	55–60	

HOW TO INTERPRET YOUR SCORES

The descriptions that follow are based on descriptions of the general population. Remember that this is not a definitive description of you because the questions did not ask about all the possible situations in which you might display a particular behaviour. Also, your own mood and recent experiences can adversely affect the results on a personality test.

Emotionality

This relates to the extent to which an individual can retain some emotional detachment from what is going on around them. Low scorers tend to be better able to stay calm in high-pressure situations and typically they report that they are patient and relaxed people. Scorers towards the more emotionally reactive end of the scale typically report that they can be more easily frustrated or upset, and can be prone to being restless or impatient. High scorers may also be more prone to becoming angry or losing their temper, especially when feeling under pressure.

Assertiveness

This relates to how an individual will stand up for their own rights. High scorers tend to be more assertive individuals and will typically report that they do not feel comfortable taking orders or instructions from other people, and are prepared to challenge other people if they see the need. Low scorers tend to be more co-operative and less forceful by nature, and they typically report that they would prefer to avoid confrontation and would seek to resolve conflict by co-operation rather than aggression. While high scorers can sometimes be aggressive, low scorers may be more prone to going along with something with which they are not happy because they do not feel comfortable challenging it.

Enthusiasm

This relates to how spontaneous or lively a person is. High scorers tend to be more spontaneous and enthusiastic about things, while low scorers will typically report that they are more serious and cautious by nature. While high scorers are often seen as the 'life and soul of the party' they can also be prone to acting on the spur of the moment, and can become easily bored with the routine or mundane. Low scorers may be seen as reliable and steady people, who give considered thought to their actions. They may be less willing to take risks and may be seen by others as serious and restrained.

Social Confidence

This relates to how confident and comfortable a person feels in social situations. High scorers tend to be socially confident and outgoing people who report that they are happy to be the centre of attention in social situations, and are comfortable in social situations where they do not know anybody. Low scorers are more socially reserved and they typically report that they can feel self-conscious and shy in social situations. High scorers can sometimes be perceived as overbearing, while low scorers can feel awkward or embarrassed if they suddenly become the centre of attention.

Rule Orientation

This relates to how an individual feels about rules and regulations. High scorers typically report that they take rules and regulations very seriously, and dislike seeing other people not adhering to them. Low scorers are less likely to report that they are always going to follow rules and regulations, and may on occasion view them as a hindrance. While high scorers are often seen as very conscientious people, low scorers may be more prepared to bend rules which they think are unnecessary, to reach the ultimate goal.

Sensitivity

This relates to how sensitive a person is to what other people say and do. High scorers tend to be more sensitive and report that they can be hurt or upset if someone criticizes them. Low scorers tend to be more objective and will typically report that they prefer to deal with matters from a logical rather than an emotional viewpoint. While high scorers can be very sensitive to, and concerned with other people's feelings, they may be prone to being more subjective in outlook. Low scorers, on the other hand, are more objective by nature but may be prone to overlooking people's feelings when making decisions that affect them.

Caution

This relates to how trusting and accepting a person is of other people. High scorers tend to report that they are more cautious about accepting people at face value, and more questioning of their motives. Low scorers report that they are happier to trust the people they meet without too much question, and spend less time worrying whether people have ulterior motives. While it is harder to deceive high scorers because they tend to be more wary of others, low scorers tend to be more at risk of being taken advantage of by others because of their trusting nature and positive view of other people.

Cognitive style

This refers to a person's intellectual style, rather than their ability, and is to do with the way a person perceives and takes in information about the world around them in order to make decisions and solve problems. High scorers tend to be more abstract and imaginative in their thinking style, preferring to look for patterns in information. Low scorers tend to report that they are more concrete in their thinking style, preferring to focus on the practical realities of problem solving in the real world. In their desire to see the 'big picture', high scorers may be prone to overlooking the fine detail of a situation, while low scorers may not always seek to look beyond what is immediately apparent.

Openness to others

This is to do with how open a person is with other people. High scorers typically report that they are comfortable sharing information about themselves, particularly about their thoughts and feelings, with other people. Low scorers report that they are more private by nature and prefer to keep their own thoughts and feelings to themselves. High scorers tend to be viewed as being easier to get to know, as they are happier to engage in self-disclosure. Low scorers may be perceived as being more distant because of their reticence to readily divulge things about themselves.

Self-Esteem

This is to do with the general level of background tension or anxiety a person feels without any environmental stimulation. High scorers tend to report that they are relaxed by nature and quite confident in their own abilities. They are not particularly prone to worrying about things, and for the most part feel satisfied with themselves. Low scorers are more prone to worrying about things and feeling anxious. Low scorers also report that they tend to feel responsible for things when they go wrong, and they can sometimes lack faith in their own abilities, even when there is no externally verifiable reason for them to do so. High scorers can be resilient people who feel in control over what happens to them, low scorers can be more prone to self-doubt and feeling vulnerable.

Adaptability

This is to do with a person's attitude towards change and uncertainty. High scorers typically report that they view change positively, and tend to enjoy the experience. Low scorers typically report that they prefer stability and are happier with the conventional and established. High scorers can often feel restricted in an environment that is unchanging and predictable, while low scorers tend to prefer a stable environment and can view change with some trepidation, preferring the established and conventional.

Independence

This factor is to do with how much a person needs to have the company of other people. High scorers tend to report that they prefer to work alone, and feel no real need for the support of others. Low scorers are more group oriented, and tend to report that they perform best when in the company of others. While high scorers can be highly independent, they can also be perceived by others as not being natural team workers. Low scorers may not enjoy an environment where they have to work in isolation, and may rely on the company of a group as a source of support.

HINTS ON DEALING WITH PERSONALITY TESTS

You will be pleased to know that no particular preparation is required for a personality test. However bear a few things in mind.

- Above all be honest! If you are not and you get a job based on your personality profile, you are unlikely to be happy in it. Supposing you paint a picture of yourself as being highly independent and self-reliant when in fact you are very team oriented. If the job entails working alone for long periods you would not be happy.
- Do not try to paint a picture of yourself that is what you think the employer is looking for. Apart from being rather dishonest, the evidence you provide during the

feedback and follow-up interview is unlikely to tie in with what you have said about yourself in the test.

- Listen to the instructions very carefully. You may be asked to answer the questions based on how you would behave at work, or how you would behave generally.
- Expect questions to which you can do nothing other than answer 'depends' or which you could answer in either direction. Don't worry about them, you should have the chance to clarify your responses at interview afterwards. The test instructions should also tell you how to deal with such questions when you come across them.
- Don't worry about individual questions too much. The level of analysis goes on at the trait rather than individual question level. Just give the best answer you can.
- Tests are designed so that it is not always apparent which particular trait is being measured by a particular question. Don't waste time thinking about this, just answer the questions as quickly as you can. The first answer that comes into your head is usually the best one.
- Personality tests are more prone to error than any other type of test because there is scope for test takers to project a less than accurate picture of themselves. When used properly, you should have a feedback and follow-up interview to see how accurate the results are. So, think about your own personality to get ready for it.

8

Dealing with Tests and the Testing Process

A test is usually just one part of a multi-stage selection process so, if you are invited to attend a test session, you can deservedly congratulate yourself for having progressed that far.

Experienced selectors will know that information suggesting conflicting characteristics often emerges from the selection process. For instance, observations made during a group exercise might suggest a particular candidate is very good at problem solving, while their performance on an aptitude test might suggest they are not. As a result, selectors and recruiters need to gather as much high-quality evidence and information as possible about those particular characteristics they are interested in.

Although the idea of multi-stage selection may seem daunting, it can also work in your favour if you apply yourself. Because it is common for organizations to use the results of a test to build an interview structure around, you should remember that the results of a test are rarely considered in isolation.

One mistaken belief is that a 'poor' performance on an ability or aptitude test will automatically rule a candidate out of further consideration for the job. Because testers know that scores on ability and aptitude tests are subject to error, and because personality tests need to be checked against information from other sources, tests are hardly ever used in isolation. When they are, it is usually with clearly defined abilities in mind, such as mechanical reasoning. Situations where the relationship between test score and work performance is as clear as this are very rare. Also, very often the testing process may include personality tests, and since these are purely descriptive in nature, in such cases there can be no such thing as a 'poor' performance.

WHAT INFORMATION IS AVAILABLE ABOUT TESTS?

If you have been expressly told that testing is to be part of the recruitment process, the company may divulge which types of test are to be used, although only rarely will they identify the actual tests.

Beyond this, it is possible to obtain short practice test items and familiarization materials from some test publishers. There are also a number of books like this one containing sample tests. A lot of additional information is in circulation about tests, but it tends to be technical in nature and is most often found in dedicated trade journals. The Internet also has a great deal of test related information, but be warned – much of it is purely speculative or opinion presented as fact. There are details at the end of this book of some reputable sources of information on testing.

INTRODUCING COMPETENCY-BASED INTERVIEWS

In the 'bad old days' of selection, the whole process tended to consist of an unstructured interview in which the interviewer(s) and the interviewee engaged in a freewheeling unstructured social interaction, with each modifying their comments in response to those of the other. No two interviews were the same, even for the same job, and this left the interviewer in the position of trying to compare chalk and cheese. Because of this, many interviewers would simply go on 'gut instinct'.

In the 1980s, interviewing underwent something of a revolution. Out went unstructured interviews and in came interviews in which the questions asked were based on those characteristics shown to be relevant to work performance.

This had one immediate effect – it removed from the process the opportunity for both the interviewer and interviewee to manipulate the process to their own advantage by introducing irrelevant information. The next step in this process was to take a step back from what the candidate was like underneath and look at what they were like on the surface, at their actual behaviours.

When one thinks about it, this is entirely logical. If you want to know how well someone can work with other people, which one of these would you do:

a) Ask them, 'Well can you work with other people?'
b) Watch them working with other people.

In an interview situation, one would hardly expect the interviewee to respond, 'Not very well really!' But, if you were to actually ask them to take part in an exercise that required them to work with other people, you would be able to see for yourself.

Since this is not always practical, a compromise has to be reached, and this compromise is a 'competency-based interview'. Here, the interviewee will be asked to provide examples of when they have demonstrated a particular behaviour. While this may not be as good as actually watching working practice, it is a lot better than simply asking the interviewee if they are any good at something. Now, the interviewer would ask:

'Can you tell me about a time when you had to complete a task under pressure?'

These days, all good selection is competency based.

PREPARING FOR A TEST SESSION

- When you are invited to a test session, you may be asked if you have a disability. If you are not asked, and you do have a disability or a condition that you think could affect your performance, be sure to tell the test administrator well in advance. Many tests come in different forms, helping to make them suitable for use with people who have certain types of disability (for instance, large print versions for those who may have a visual impairment).
- If you wear spectacles or a hearing aid, bring them with you.
- Get a good night's sleep beforehand – not always easy, but try. Some light exercise before going to bed often helps, also avoid eating heavy meals or drinking beverages containing caffeine in the three or four hours before you go to bed. Alcohol should always be avoided as it can disturb normal sleep patterns.
- On the morning of the test, eat breakfast, even if you are nervous and do not feel like eating. Failure to do so can lower your glucose levels and drastically reduce your performance.
- Avoid caffeine and alcohol before taking the test. Caffeine will increase alertness but can decrease concentration, while alcohol may seem like a stimulant but in reality acts as a depressant on the nervous system. Caffeine and alcohol will also dehydrate you.
- Make your travel arrangements well in advance, and have a contingency plan ready just in case. Nothing will upset you more than having to rush to make it to the test session on time.
- Make sure you know where you are to report for the test. Do not be afraid to call the organization carrying out the testing for directions.
- Listen to the test administrator's instructions carefully,

and ask if you are not sure you understand what is expected of you. Don't feel foolish, you may be the only person brave enough to ask, but I can guarantee you will not be the only person who wants to.

- Immediately before going into the test, keep calm, take a few deep breaths, and talk to other candidates to keep your mind off what is about to happen.
- Remember that psychometric tests are rarely tests of pure knowledge, and although some basic verbal or mathematical ability tends to be assumed, a lack of revision is unlikely to do you too much harm.
- Remember that tests are designed so that you are unlikely to be able to answer all of the questions correctly in the time allowed. With ability and aptitude tests this is supposed to happen, so don't start panicking halfway through the test if you think you are running out of time. You will run out of time – I can guarantee it.
- Tests tend not to penalize you for incorrect answers, so don't be frightened to take a best guess if you have a reasonable idea what the correct answer is.
- Pay close attention to the administrator's instructions on how to do the test. If you are really stuck on a question and don't know what to do, go back over the examples which most tests provide in the front of the question booklet.
- Don't spend too much time on any one question. You will quickly get a feel for how long a single question should take.
- Although questions within a test can vary in difficulty, just move on if you really get stuck. Unless you are specifically instructed to go through the questions in a specific order, it may be useful to work through once very quickly to try and identify those that are easier.
- With all tests, if you really cannot establish what the correct answer is, a good approach is to identify those answers that are clearly incorrect and eliminate them.

Then, if you are reduced to guessing, at least you have improved your chances of arriving at the right answer.

- If you do find yourself with some free time at the end of the test use it to double-check your answers.
- If you are allowed to use rough paper for working out, use it.
- Mark your answers clearly and in the correct manner, and only change an answer in the correct manner. With a carbon-backed answer sheet the correct answers will be printed on the rearmost sheet and using an eraser will make it illegible, although the top sheet may look fine. This is another reason to pay attention when the instructions are being read out.
- Write your own test questions, this is an excellent way of practising.
- Practise, practise, practise.

THE TEST SESSION

During the test session itself, you can simply hand yourself over to the administrator and let them do the work. They will have been doing a lot of preparation themselves beforehand. If there are more than about eight candidates to be tested in any one session, you will usually find that there is more than one administrator.

Most people are nervous about psychometric testing, and experienced test administrators know it is important to relax candidates as much as possible. Nervous candidates may perform poorly on account of their nerves, or they may even fail to turn up for the test session.

Testing is quite a formal procedure and the administrator will generally use the introduction to the session to build up a rapport with you and to relax you. The introduction to the test session is not a rigorously standardized procedure and is often no more than an informal chat. At this point, you should take advantage of any opportunity to ask any questions you may have – and for a final visit to the lavatory! Once the administrator has dealt with any last minute questions, they will begin the test administration itself.

Do not be put off if the administrator seems less friendly at this point. It is because they will now be reading from a set of standardized instructions. You will usually have the chance to do some practice examples that are not normally scored and are used to ensure that everybody understands the question format and that they are using the correct answer procedure. Listen to the instructions carefully and concentrate on what you are being asked to do.

The administrator will usually wander around the room during the practice questions to check that everybody is doing the examples correctly. They should then explain what is required of you during the test and how long you will have. If nobody has any more questions they will then begin the test.

Once the test begins it will usually be carried out under normal exam conditions. This means that no talking will be allowed. If you have any questions about the test once the test begins you will only be directed to the examples and instructions. The administrator will not explain aspects of specific questions to you, nor do anything which might put the other candidates at a disadvantage.

When the test finishes you will be told to stop writing immediately. If you are seen continuing after the time is up then your answers may not be counted. Remember that this is just like an exam. You will not be allowed to move until the test materials have been collected and you must never attempt to remove test materials from the test session.

Usually, you will be thanked for your participation and the next stages in the process explained to you. With an immense sense of relief and an unshakeable conviction that you have done terribly, you are now free to go. This is only a general description of the process involved and it will vary depending on the type and number of tests being used, as well as the number of candidates being tested.

DEALING WITH POST-TEST FEEDBACK AND INTERVIEW

Once the tests have been scored, you should be invited for an interview. Usually, test scoring takes a day or so to complete and if the selection process is complex or if it involved a large number of candidates, then it may be a week or more before you hear anything.

Although the main function of this interview is to provide you with feedback on your test performance, we should not forget that it may also be used to gather evidence to support or refute the evidence already gained during the selection process. It is rare to have a purely feedback- or development-oriented interview, although if you are an internal candidate this is more likely since organizations will be aware that unsuccessful internal candidates can become de-motivated if they are not handled correctly. If you are an external candidate, then the exact format of the interview will depend on when in the process you sat the test. It may be focused on just gathering evidence to support the information that emerged from the test, or it may have a wider function such as discussing terms and conditions as well.

If the interview follows testing, the line of questioning is likely to be focused around the types of trait for which you have been tested and it is here that a candidate might be asked about specific occasions when they had demonstrated particular kinds of behaviour. The interviewer will be bearing in mind that the test score will be prone to error. They will also be aware that if the error has been large enough and they were to base a decision on whether or not to offer someone a job, they would be likely to either

let a potentially excellent employee go, or employ someone who may not be up to the demands of the role.

Even if you are being interviewed immediately after
you have been tested and you are fairly certain that the interviewer does not have the results of your tests to hand,
they will still be likely to ask about the same areas. Many
selection procedures involve the use of an 'assessment
matrix' which the assessors will use to record the information about particular characteristics measured using different tools. In the example below, you will see that all of the
characteristics are assessed using more than one method.
Where a certain assessment tool is used to assess a particular characteristic, this is denoted by an 'X' and a numerical
score is often used to describe a person's performance on a
particular skill as assessed by a particular tool. These
scores can then be added up or averaged to produce an
overall performance score. Clearly, this cannot be done
until the scores from all of the assessment tools used have
been gathered.

Assessment Method

	Interview	Group Exercise	Presentation	Psychometric Test
Assertiveness	X	X		X
Sensitivity	X	X		X
Problem solving		X	X	X
Team working		X		X
Communication Skills	X	X	X	

Remember that the selection process is not about testing.
It is about obtaining information about particular characteristics of the candidate and the test is just one tool used
to do this. This means that, even if you do poorly on a particular task or test, you will often have the chance to redeem
yourself. It also means that, just because a numerical

reasoning test is over, it does not mean the assessment of your numerical reasoning ability is over as well.

STRUCTURE OF THE FEEDBACK SESSION

Although the exact content of the feedback session will vary, it is likely to include some of the following elements.

- Because testing can be very stressful and there are often significant consequences for the candidate, a *developmental* rather than judgmental approach is normally adopted. Poorly delivered feedback might cause a candidate to withdraw from the selection process and often a good starting point is to ask the candidate what they thought of the test, the test session and the process so far.
- During feedback, it will usually be taken for granted that you have very little knowledge of testing. You might be asked if you have done any tests before and what feedback you received then.
- After questioning to examine your understanding of the ideas of reliability, validity, norm groups, standard scores and so on, the interviewer will adopt one of the standard scoring methods and deliver your feedback to you using that. The simplest approach is often the best and they may well adopt something straightforward like a five point grading system, such as:

A – well above average
B – above average
C – average
D – below average
E – well below average.

They should also describe to you the nature of the norm or comparison group they are using, as well as the nature of the trait that the test was used to measure.

- Finally, the consequences and implications of obtaining a particular score should be explained to you. This might include how the score fits into the other information obtained about you. If there are any discrepancies they should be explored. Again, be prepared to support what has emerged from the test process (as well as from any other selection tools) with evidence.

AND, FINALLY ...

The world of psychometric testing has not really changed much over the last 20–30 years. Most of the things we know now we knew then.

The major developments in the field have come about with the advent of Internet and computer-based testing. This does not mean that the tests themselves have got any better, but it does mean that the methods of administering and scoring them have. These new administration options and the instantaneous scoring and report writing they offer also mean that you are more likely than ever to be asked to sit a test, especially a 'general purpose' one such as a personality test.

On-line recruitment has also taken off in a big way and it may not be long before it becomes a standard requirement to sit a test when applying for a job. But, all that has changed is the administration method, and the requirement to seek supporting evidence is still there. Whether you are tested on-line or at an assessment centre, do always remember that decisions are rarely based on test results alone. So don't panic, but prepare thoroughly!

Appendix 1
Answers to the Tests

CHAPTER 2 – TESTS OF NUMERICAL ABILITY

Test 1 (Addition)

1	52
2	36
3	66
4	252
5	18
6	199
7	61
8	106
9	123
10	96
11	58
12	39
13	116
14	35
15	24
16	31
17	23
18	22
19	22
20	50
21	179
22	53

23	166
24	178
25	77
26	101
27	54
28	80
29	47
30	35

Test 2 (Subtraction)

1	–95
2	–4
3	–88
4	–78
5	–70
6	14
7	–23
8	8
9	–16
10	104
11	–26
12	167
13	–21
14	–19
15	33
16	27
17	–128
18	–79
19	39
20	–213
21	–40
22	182
23	–27
24	–111
25	–14
26	27

27	28
28	20
29	30
30	91

Test 3 (Division)

1	3
2	5
3	6
4	3
5	5
6	4
7	3
8	3
9	1
10	10
11	20
12	3
13	6
14	11
15	61
16	19
17	10
18	2
19	4
20	9
21	17
22	10
23	37
24	20
25	5
26	50
27	5
28	30
29	11
30	8

Test 4 (Multiplication)

1 72
2 85
3 80
4 207
5 119
6 90
7 254
8 72
9 225
10 260
11 288
12 320
13 132
14 918
15 65
16 720
17 152
18 180
19 300
20 245
21 108
22 84
23 117
24 250
25 148
26 91
27 140
28 405
29 600
30 275

Test 5 (Combination)

1 41
2 10
3 1

4	10
5	44
6	80
7	126
8	10
9	370
10	800
11	290
12	5
13	23
14	144
15	50
16	10
17	128
18	4
19	1
20	430
21	210
22	200
23	2
24	36
25	73
26	2
27	0
28	60
29	127
30	24

Test 6 (Combination – Percentages and Fractions, Series, Equations)

(Note: although you weren't told, there were no (e) answers. The correct answer was always there.)

1	b)
2	c)
3	c)

4	b)
5	b)
6	b)
7	b)
8	d)
9	d)
10	b)
11	b)
12	d)
13	d)
14	a)
15	c)
16	c)
17	d)
18	b)
19	c)
20	b)
21	d) (this follows the sequence: +1, x2, +3, x4, +5 ...)
22	c)
23	c)
24	b)
25	a)
26	a)
27	b)
28	b)
29	d)
30	a)

Test 7 (Number series)

1 a) The numbers increase by 1 each time.
2 c) The numbers double each time.
3 b) The numbers decrease by 1 each time.
4 d) The numbers follow the sequence: + 1, – 2, + 1 ...
5 a) The numbers follow the sequence: + 1, ÷ 2, + 1 ...
6 a) The numbers follow the sequence: + 3, – 3, + 3 ...
7 c) The numbers follow the sequence: x 4, + 4, x 4 ...

8 a) The numbers follow the sequence: x 2 ...

9 b) The numbers follow the sequence: x 1, x 2, x 1 ...

10 b) The numbers follow the sequence: x 3, x 2, x 3 ...

11 c) The numbers follow the sequence: + 5, – 5, + 5 ...

12 d) The numbers follow the sequence: + 1, + 2, + 3 ...

13 a) The numbers follow the sequence: + 1, – 1, + 1 ...

14 d) The numbers follow the sequence: x 1, x 2, x 3 ...

15 b) Each number is multiplied by itself.

16 d) The numbers follow the sequence: + 2, x 2, + 2 ...

17 b) The numbers follow the sequence: – 5, x 5, – 5 ...

18 b) The numbers follow the sequence: – 2, – 4, – 6 ...

19 c) The numbers follow the sequence: ÷ 1, ÷ 2, ÷ 1 ...

20 b) The numbers follow the sequence: ÷ itself, x itself, ÷ itself ...

Test 8 (Numerical Problem Solving)

1 i) c)

ii) c)

iii) c)

iv) d)

v) a)

vi) c)

2 i) c)

ii) c)

iii c)

iv) b)

v) a)

vi) d)

vii d)

viii) b)

ix) c)

x) c)

xi) a)

3 i) c)
   ii) b)
   iii) b)
   iv) c)
   v) b)
   vi) c)
   vii) c)
   viii) a)
   ix) b)

4 i) c)
   ii) a)
   iii) c)
   iv) c)
   v) c)
   vi) c)
   vii) a)

5 i) b)
   ii) b)
   iii) a)
   iv) a)
   v) b)
   vi) c)
   vii) a)

CHAPTER 3 – TESTS OF VERBAL ABILITY

Test 1 (Spelling)

1 c)
2 a)
3 e)
4 d)
5 c)
6 c)
7 a)

8	d)
9	a)
10	e)
11	d)
12	a)
13	a)
14	e)
15	e)
16	b)
17	d)
18	a)
19	d)
20	e)
21	d)
22	a)
23	e)
24	a)
25	d)
26	b)
27	e)
28	e)
29	e)
30	c)
31	b)
32	d)
33	c)
34	e)
35	c)
36	e)
37	a)
38	c)
39	d)
40	d)

Test 3 – Comprehension (Related Words)

Test 2 – Comprehension (Missing Words)

Note: while some of the words in each question could, in theory, be used to complete the sentence, only the one that helps it make the most sense is the correct answer.

1 b)
2 d)
3 c)
4 a)
5 a)
6 d)
7 c)
8 d)
9 c)
10 a)
11 d)
12 d)
13 b)
14 c)
15 b)
16 a)
17 d)
18 b)
19 d)
20 b)

Test 3 – Comprehension (Related Words)

1 a)
2 c)
3 a)
4 d)
5 b)
6 a)
7 d)
8 a)
9 e)

10	c)
11	b)
12	c)
13	e)
14	e)
15	d)
16	a)
17	b)
18	c)
19	d)
20	a)
21	c)
22	b)
23	b)
24	c)
25	b)

Test 4 – Comprehension (Related Words)

1   d) the others involve actions with the eyes
2   b) the others involve disposing of something
3   a) the others refer to specific time periods
4   e) they are all objects which can hold things
5   a) the others refer to emotional not physical feelings
6   a) the others are things which can be read
7   b) the others are actions
8   a) the others are all designed to sit on
9   d) the others are specific types of building
10 b) the others describe light
11 b) the others are all actions
12 c) the others can be used to stick things together
13 e) they all refer to the same thing
14 a) the others are all engine driven
15 d) the others describe noise rather than being a source of noise
16 e) they all refer to the same thing
17 e) they all refer to the same thing

18	c) the others are all domestic pets
19	b) the others are all actions, joy is an emotion
20	d) the others all describe snow
21	c) the others are all fish
22	c) the others are specific colours
23	d) the others are all vocal in nature
24	d) the others refer to specific periods of time
25	d) the others are sources of brightness

Test 5 – Comprehension (Related Words)

1	a)
2	c)
3	a)
4	c)
5	a)
6	d)
7	b)
8	d)
9	a)
10	c)
11	a)
12	d)
13	e)
14	a)
15	e)
16	b)
17	e)
18	d)
19	c)
20	a)

Test 6 – Comprehension (Synonyms and Antonyms)

1	a)
2	c)
3	a)
4	b)

5   b)
6   d)
7   a)
8   a)
9   a)
10 a)
11 e)
12 b)
13 d)
14 a)
15 a)
16 d)
17 b)
18 d)
19 a)
20 e)
21 b)
22 e)
23 d)
24 a)
25 e)

Test 7 – Problem Solving (Critical Thinking)

1   i) c)
    ii) a)
    iii) b)
    iv) c)
    v) c)
    vi) a)
    vii) c)
    viii) c)
    ix) b)
    x) c)

2   i) a)
    ii) c)

iii) a)
iv) c)
v) b)
vi) c)
vii) c)
viii) b)
ix) c)
x) c)

3   i) a)
   ii) b)
   iii) a)
   iv) b)
   v) c)
   vi) b)
   vii) a)
   viii) c)
   ix) b)
   x) b)

4   i) c)
   ii) c)
   iii) a)
   iv) b)
   v) c)
   vi) c)
   vii) b)
   viii) c)
   ix) b)
   x) c)

5   i) a)
   ii) c)
   iii) c)
   iv) b)
   v) b)

CHAPTER 4 – TESTS OF ABSTRACT ABILITY

Test 1 – Pattern Series

1   c) the number in the top right of each figure refers to the number of sides the shape in the same figure has. In the case of figure one, ∞ refers to infinity.

2   b) the arrows rotate 90 degrees clockwise, the shaded and unshaded triangles alternate and the number of dashes increase by one each time.

3   b) the number marks on the diagonal centre line alternate between one and two, and the shaded and unshaded circles alternate positions each time.

4   d) the large central + and – signs alternate, as do the small + and – signs in the top left, the small circle remains unchanged.

5   b) the numbers alternate top and bottom left and increase by one each time.

6   a) the triangle and circle move as a pair clockwise around the figure, one square at a time.

7   c) the shaded column moves across the figure one column at a time and returns to the start, the shaded circle maintains its column but alternates between a position at the top and a position at the bottom of the column.

8   c) the lower sector of the large circle alternates between shaded and unshaded, the * and A figures alternate, and the small shaded circle moves around the figure in a clockwise direction one corner at a time.

9   d) the small square alternates between shaded and unshaded, the number of marks in the top left increases

by one each time and the arrow in the bottom right rotates clockwise through 90 degrees each time.

10   a) the figure gains a new side each time, gradually increasing in size.

11   b) the numbers increase by 2 each time and alternate between being inside a circle or not, the figure in the bottom right has another two arms added each time.

12   d) the figures alternate the shading between top and bottom each time, and increase by one alternating shaded and unshaded each time.

13   e) there is no rule at work here, although you may well upon closer inspection find some subtle ones of your own design.

14   a) the arrows alternate between pointing up and down and between being inside a circle or a square, the letter increases by one each time and moves clockwise around the corners of the figure.

15   e) there is no rule at work here, although you may well upon closer inspection find some subtle ones of your own design.

16   d) the circles moves down the line in stages alternating between shaded and unshaded, the dots gradually move round the corners increasing in number by one each time.

17   a) the central shape alternates between shaded and unshaded, the arrow in the top right moves from left to right, the arrow in the bottom left does not move.

18   d) the top left circle alternates between shaded and unshaded, the * figure alternates between the same two diagonals and the smaller number multiplied by itself produces the larger number.

19   a) the figure increases the number of its arms by one each time.

20   a) the central shape alternates between shaded and unshaded, the column of spheres increases by two each time as well as alternating sides, as does the + or – which alternates in both sign and side.

Test 2 – Related Symbols (Odd One Out)

1   c) this is the only figure with an odd number of shaded circles.

2   e) this is the only figure with an odd number of smaller symbols, the others all have four.

3   d) the other figures all have a small and a large version on the same symbol.

4   b) this is the only figure where the small black symbol is not centrally placed.

5   c) this is the only figure where the circle is in a corner rather than in the centre.

6   d) the numbers in the other figures all correlate with the number of small shapes in that figure.

7   e) this one is a bit sneaky and really makes you think – it is actually very dependent on numerical ability, but because abstract reasoning is to do with problem solving you should eventually arrive at the correct answer. All of the figures contain two numbers, the smaller of which will divide exactly into the larger.

8   d) the smaller shape in the other figures is the same as the larger shape.

9   e) the arrow in the other figures points at the smaller symbol in the figure.

10 c) the other figures contain only complete steps.

11 e) if the larger shape is partially shaded then it is the same shape as the smaller shape.

12 e) the other figures all have an even number of smaller shapes in the central area.

13 e) this is a very subtle one – this is the only figure where the cross extends beyond the confines of the circle.

14 d) this figure is the only face with both eyes closed.

15 c) this figure has an odd number of protrusions.

16 e) this is the only figure where the two shaded corners are not opposite to each other.

17 e) in the other figures the number refers to the position of the letter in the alphabet.

18 e) another subtle one – the shaded square should be opposite the shaded circle.

19 a) this is the only figure where the shaded portions of the grid are adjacent to each other.

20 c) adding the number of sides in both figures produces an even number of sides, the other produces an odd number.

CHAPTER 5 – TESTS OF TECHNICAL ABILITY

Mechanical Ability Test 1

1 b) as the load on the left is heavier than the load on the right the plank will not balance in the centre. The additional weight of the plank will mean that it will balance nearer the heavier load.

2 c) The longer handle will allow greater leverage. The additional purchase provided on the nut by b) will not affect how much force can be applied to the nut.

3 c) the larger wheel size will allow the wheels to rotate faster than a smaller wheel size.

4 c) the multiple pulleys mean that while each pull on rope 'A' will result in a smaller raising of the load the effort required will be less. Effectively, this works like a gearing mechanism.

5 b) the deflated wheel will provide a larger surface area over which to distribute the weight.

6 b) while a) may be easier to grip than c), b) requires no gripping so all of the force applied can be used to rotate the nut.

7 a) this container has the largest surface area of liquid.

8 b) the bracing members provide both lateral and vertical strengthening of the tower, the other two brace the tower in only one direction.

9 a) the amount of water in a) can be estimated as being less than in b) or c) so for the same amount of water to flow through all 3 channels it must flow more quickly through a) as it holds less volume.

10   c) a vertical load placed on this fixing will drive the nail further into the wall if it slips.

11   c) provides the largest force concentrated into the smallest surface area.

12   a) X and Y will light because X is already part of a closed circuit, closing the switch A will also complete the circuit for Y.

13   a) the coiled band indicates that it was wound anti-clockwise, when it unwinds it will drive the propeller clockwise.

14   c) it weighs the most, irrespective of what it is made of.

15   b) wheel B will turn anticlockwise, you can trace the movement around.

16   c) because it has the most wax.

17   c) the longest wire will produce the longest wavelength and a longer wavelength produces a lower note.

18   c) the pressure of the water will force the porthole against the entire window seal, with a) and b) the water could push the window through as the hull provides nothing to push against.

19   a) the bullet will not bounce off at exactly the same angle because some of its forward momentum will be absorbed on impact. It will not bounce off at the lesser angle c).

20   a) you can follow the movement through the mechanism.

21   a) any gas increases in volume as the pressure around it decreases which is what happens as you rise through the atmosphere.

22   c) provides the largest surface area to resist the action of surface waves by providing resistance in the water.

23   a) it has the largest mass of water directly above it.

24   a) the load is most evenly spread and lowers the centre of gravity of the vessel which makes it more stable.

25 a) the load is borne mostly by the wheels of the barrow because it is directly over them.

26 a) although this is a geometry question the answer can be seen by drawing a line from each point to the moon, this represents a line of sight.

27 c) has the narrowest focus, the beam will be smaller but sharper.

28 a) this would have the largest force concentrated onto the smallest surface area.

29 d) the determining factor is the size of object A, which is the same in each case, so the amount of water object A displaces is the same, irrespective of the amount of water it is dropped into.

30 b) provides the largest surface area for the water to evaporate from and the largest surface area to absorb heat from the flame.

Spatial Test 1 – Constructing Objects

1 b)
2 a)
3 b)
4 d)
5 c)
6 a)
7 c)
8 b)
9 a)
10 b)
11 a)
12 a)
13 d)
14 a)
15 b)
16 a)
17 a)
18 d)

19 c)
20 b)
21 a)
22 b)
23 c)
24 a)
25 b)
26 b)
27 d)
28 b)
29 b)
30 d)

Spatial Test 2 – Rotating Objects

1 e)
2 c)
3 e)
4 c)
5 d)
6 a)
7 e)
8 a)
9 c)
10 d)
11 a)
12 a)
13 a)
14 a)
15 a)
16 b)
17 a)
18 d)
19 e)
20 c)

CHAPTER 6 – TESTS OF SPEED AND PERCEPTION

Test 1 – Checking Information

	Column 1	Column 2
1	MæYy6++aT†š&	MæY6++aT†š&
2	XnP¢Ÿþl'1'''X	XnP¢Ÿþ**1'''X
3	þ(¹¸Ö|=ãaf?a	þ(¹¸Ö|=ãaf?a
4	hÚý>aÔmgŸDÓ	hÚý>aÔmHŸDÓ
5	ÌVÅÊa□%"ÜÊ$'	ÌVÅÊa□%"ÜÊ$'
6	"ª(;a®X¯˜»ýª	"ª(;a®X¯˜»ýª
7	Š¸Ö·OëOò&To×	Š¸Ö·OYTò&To×
8	ú×üÎ2ûMÓ¢ø¥á	ú×üÎ2ûMÓ¢ø¥á
9	"°μ□+aSûa,*a	"°μ□/*Sûa,*a
10	ÛaXÆ<±□"aÎ¼c	ÛaXÆ<±□ƒ*¹¼c
11	å$t5ËëÑê1ßêí	å$t5ËëÑê1ßêí
12	auke§i~3□æéî	Auke$"~3□æéî
13	–š{KX[KŠS$□«	–š{KX[KŠS$□«
14	|P]J³aaarflm	|P]J³Aearflm
15	f¯[¢|5mýy•*I	f¯[¢|5mýy•*I
16	ÿ ^G']A¨ë>aø	ÿ ^G']A¨ë>aø
17	□□iªZø...u=·"G	□□iªZø...□=·"G
18	Óša[›...,u&/ßJ	Óša[›...,u&/ßJ
19	g"†Š6uã÷q¸ÈÊ	g"†Š6uã÷q¸ÊÊ
20	□-gsoyiåœñ\[	□-gsoyiåœñ\[
21	OaÉaÑ8t'aeYX	OaÉaÑ8t'aeYX
22	pAaaGZ–Š™Ï˜p	PAaaGZ+Š™Ï˜p
23	‡)à¾aÂ∂·@aañ	‡)à¾aÂ∂·@aañ
24	/öŸ‹âÒm%²Òa^	/öŸ‹âÒm£$Òa^
25	%¼W¹½HÑÒ&³iYa	%¼W¹½HÑÒ&³iYa
26	aŠ7a‹å(.a"□×	aŠ7a‹å(.a"□×
27	³×¼Sý™â□^Ïþa	³×¼Sý™â□^Ïþa
28	□ax?dñ□°Å®éμ	□aX?dñ□°Å®éμ

29	aÁaûH?h‡])ÿ,G	aÁaûH?h‡])ÿ,G
30	Ìanãjú=a✧«&î	Ìanãjú=a✧«&î
31	×õ÷aa.*Éÿayã	×õ÷aa.*Éÿayã
32	^a³/₄³Ð<3á«µñ❑	^a³/₄³Ð<3á«µñ❑
33	fá-FaØi÷ʹë¶¥	fá-ft Øi÷ʹë¶¥
34	£fµa)❑3çBa±È	£fµa)❑3çBa±È
35	ó,©;aüV¥Ô5a;	ó,©;aüV¥Ô5a;
36	VÒµé⁻4aaé×>a	VÒµé⁻4 ee é×>a
37	²†OajÅ✧†ÒmÒ<	²†OajÅ✧†ÒmÒ<
38	Ö±°ša…Â›pT❑d	Ö±°ša…Â›pT❑d
39	a.aî[o-ÑC-w{	a.aî[o-ÑC-w{
40	❑ap*6V¿õ÷❑]ᵢ	❑ap*6V¿õ */]ᵢ
41	Çÿ aâxWRña×Ù	Çÿ aâxWRña×Ù
42	ôKH5?ô‹Ëo±ÛÚ	ôKH5?ô‹Ëo±ÛÚ
43	M5Äf×÷Liöday	M5Äf×÷Liöday
44	ÑG¹/₄‚ŠÂ#±ŸË;?	ÑG¹/₄‚ŠÂ#±ŸË;?
45	§Òîõaaɤ̀èËaØg	§Òîõaaɤ̀e ËaØg
46	ña›aÅaÄ″µ❑¡I	ña›aÅaÄ″µ❑¡I
47	a❑,;apã!÷na†	a❑,;apã!÷na†
48	a÷aT°—Oúër£K	a÷ e4°—Oúër£K
49	• ̄ë¥❑aSÿ ʹ±á	• ̄ë¥❑aSÿ ʹ±á
50	ÿûajÝú?O®GÄ7	ÝûajÝú ‹ O®GÄ7
51	a°o‹lQa©⁻øoN	a°o‹lQa©⁻øoN
52	¶Õ✧‰,íu}aKÙu	¶Õ✧‰,íu}aKÙu
53	aamaaaÛ:y£Í3	Aaamaa Û:y£Í3
54	❑³ᵃ³a″¶?l»½Z	❑³ᵃ³a″¶?l»½Z
55	Š#S—úó‚JŸ7aê	Š#S—úó‚JŸ7aê
56	Ö<°Y❑áaþÊš÷Ç	Ö<°Y❑áaþÊš÷Ç
57	Z^‡¬Í¡YYΦÉâk	Z^‡¬Í¡YY Y Éâk
58	mÿjò<Âaa\¢™C	mÿjò<Âaa\¢™C
59	K/˜aʹãtgaÏ©£	K/˜aʹãtga Í©£
60	Ë¿ÄΦa³/₄″HþÂSã	Ë¿Ä Pa³/₄″HþÂSã

Test 2 – Checking Information

	Column 1	Column 2
1	Mr P S Bowman 76 Agriola St Acton London Order ref: 57945A	Mr P S Bowman 76 Agricola St Acton London Order ref: 57945A
2	Ms C A Howey 98 Sunderland Road Esprick Surrey Order ref: 134922B	Ms C A Howey 98 Sunderland Road Esprisk Surrey Order ref: 13922B
3	Ms C D West 24 Clifton Avenue East Creech Northants Order ref: 4457Z	Ms C D West 24 Clifton Avenue East Creach Northhants Order ref: 4457Z
4	Mrs J Chapmund 1 Coatsworth Road Fulsworth Manchester Order ref: 55741Z	Ms J Chapmund 1 Coatsworth Road Fulworth Manchester Order ref: 554171Z
5	Mr ER Hardy Salisbury House Kentbridge Walk Galsworthy East Sussex Order ref: 9754112A	Mr ER Hardy Sailisbury House Kentsbridge Walk Galsworthy East Sussex Order ref: 975412A
6	Mrs B Ledon 11a Cambridge Ave Matland Avon Order ref: 32145A	Mrs B Ledon 11a Cambridge Ave Maitland Avon Order ref: 31245A

7	Ms Madine	Mrs Madine
	12b Bexhill Rd	12b Bexhill Rd
	Musbury	Muxbury
	Lancashire	Lancashire
	Order ref: 2251A	Order ref: 21251A

8	Mr S Patterson	Mr S Patterson
	3 Leyburn Place	3 Layburn Place
	Polbay	Polbay
	Swansea	Swansea
	Wales	Wales
	Order ref: 122313F	Order ref: 122313F

9	Mr Oulsby	Mr Olsby
	25 Ripon St	25 Ripon St
	Sourin	Sourin
	Isle of Wight	Isle of Wight
	Order ref: 1521114A	Order ref: 152114A

10	Mrs LK Brown	Ms LK Brown
	6 Kellis lane	6 Kellis lane
	Boughwood	Boughwood
	West Yorkshire	West Yorkshire
	Order ref: 225287B	Order ref: 225287B

11	Mr Askew	Mr Askew
	2c March Court	2c March Court
	Bodney	Bodney
	Devon	Devon
	Order ref: 1534B	Order ref: 1534B

12	Mr Mulgrew	Mr Mulgrew
	33 Elm Road	33 Elm Road
	Ganarew	Glanarew
	Argyll	Argyll
	Order ref: 176585A	Order ref: 176855A

13 Mrs S Riley   Mr S Riley
    227b Milling Road   272b Milling Road
    Foulsham   Foulsham
    Chelsea   Chelsea
    London   London
    Order ref: 485799Z   Order ref: 485799A

14 Ms AM Wann   Ms AW Mann
    12 Brecon Place   12 Brecon Place
    Gaer   Gaer
    Isle of Skye   Ilse of Skye
    Order ref: 196536Z   Order ref: 196536Z

15 Ms L Marshall   Ms L Marshall
    62 Portmead Rise   62 Portmead Rise
    Lindsell   Lindsell
    Co Durham   Co Durham
    Order ref: 795455A   Order ref: 795455A

16 Ms Bennet   Ms J Bennet
    Palace House   Palace House
    Westover Place   Westover Place
    Kensington   Kensington
    London   London
    Order ref: 98561A   Order ref: 98561A

17 Mrs R Clark   Ms R Clark
    121 North Dene Court   121 North Dene Court
    Letterbreane   Letterbeane
    Somerset   Somerset
    Order ref: 87978B   Order ref: 87978B

18 Mr A Chishack   Mr A Chishack
    8a Lyne Lane   8a Lyne Lane
    Ridely   Ridely
    Northumberland   Northumberland
    Order ref: 4871FF   Order ref: 4871FF

19	Ms D Gulbrand	Ms D Guldbran
	1 Mann Court	1 Man Court
	Purslowe	Purslowe
	Cornwall	Cornwall
	Order ref: 2298147F	Order ref: 2298147F

20	Mr A Docherty	Mr AB Docherty
	1 The Larches	1 The Larches
	Rhoslan Place	Rhoslan Place
	Rimpton	Rimpton
	Lancaster	Lancaster
	Order ref: 458721B	Order ref: 458712B

21	Mr GD West	Mr GD West
	23 Meadow Lane	23 Meadow Lane
	Sutton Cross	Sutton Cross
	Willand	Willand
	Buckinghamshire	Buckinghamshire
	Order ref: 33658B	Order ref: 33658B

22	Mr Dixon	Mr Dixon
	86 Farlisle Place	86 Fairlisle Place
	Whincle	Whincle
	Aylesbury	Aylesbury
	Order ref: 45687A	Order ref: 45687A

23	Mrs JK Charlton	Mrs JK Charlton
	Plaid House	Pliad House
	Kingsway	Kingsway
	Achfary	Achfary
	West Lothian	Wets Lothian
	Order ref: 24555Z	Order ref: 24555Z

24	Ms JL Somers	Ms JL Sommers
	55b Runnymeade Road	55b Runnymeade Road
	Wilmslow	Wimslow
	Order ref: 44887A	Order ref: 44887A

25   Mr Toogood   Mr Toogood
      101 Thorntree Walk   101 Thorntree Walk
      Burholme Rise   Burholme Rise
      Etal   Etals
      Hampshire   Hampshire
      Order ref: 1165B   Order ref: 1165B

26   Mrs Leithead   Mrs Lethead
      114 Athrington Court   114 Athrington Court
      Helington   Hellington
      Inverness   Inverness
      Order ref: 11654B   Order ref: 11654B

27   Mr F Francotte   Mr F Francote
      77 Fieldside   77 Fieldside
      Longthorpe   Longthorpe
      Cambridgeshire   Cambridgeshire
      Order ref: 1158964Z   Order ref: 158964Z

28   Ms B Mossam   Ms B Mossam
      34 Myrtle Street   34 Myrtle Street
      Stichill Town   Stickill Town
      Glasgow   Glasgow
      Order ref: 19678Z   Order ref: 19678Z

29   Mr Saenger   Mr Seanger
      1 Huntcliffe Gardens   1 Huntcliffe Gardens
      Pentire Way   Penlire Way
      Wilburton   Wilburton
      Leeds   Leeds
      Order ref: 4567A   Order ref: 4567A

30   Mr MN McDonald   Mr M MacDonald
      11a Bruce Close   11a Bruce Close
      Bretby   Bretsby
      Edinburgh   Edinburgh
      Order ref: 555887B   Order ref: 555887B

Appendix 2 _____
Further Information

Some useful and objective advice on testing can be found from these three non-profit-making professional bodies:

The British Psychological Society
St Andrew's House
48 Princess Road East
Leicester LE1 7DR
Tel: 0116 254 9568
Fax: 0116 247 0787
E-mail: enquiry@bps.org.uk

The Institute of Personnel and Development
IPD House
Camp Road
London SW19 4UX
Tel: 0208 971 9000
Fax: 0208 263 3333
Web site: www.ipd.org.uk

American Psychological Association
750 First Street, NE
Washington DC 20002-4242
Tel: 800 374 2721 / 202 336 5500
Web site: www.apa.org

The Internet can also be a good source of information, but be wary of sites hosted by private individuals or organizations whose qualifications you are unable to verify.

The author's own web site: **www.psychometrics.co.uk** provides career development advice and information on psychometric testing.

How to Win at Aptitude Tests

A complete course with examples, explanations, practical tips and solutions

PAUL PELSHENKE

Aptitude tests, also known as IQ tests or psychometric tests, are being used more and more to test the suitability of job applicants and academic course candidates. This essential book will give you added confidence whenever you are faced with such tests, through examples of the types of test you might encounter, together with explanations, hints and tips.

The book contains examples of verbal, non-verbal, spatial and numerical tests, plus exercises to test your general knowledge and reasoning powers. By working through the exercises, you can prepare yourself for anything that employers or colleges might throw at you!

ISBN 0 7225 2814 0

How to Win at Aptitude Tests Volume II

IAIN MAITLAND

_____

A follow-up volume to *How to Win at Aptitude Tests*, *How to Win at Aptitude Tests Volume* II contains more examples of IQ and psychometric tests, together with exercises, hints and recommended answers.

Covering verbal, non-verbal, spatial and numerical tests, general knowlege and reasoning skills, how to recognize patterns, and how to successfully speed through the tests, this book is a must for anyone facing an aptitude test.

Iain Maitland is the author of *Franchising, Successful Business Plans in a Week* and several other successful business books.

ISBN 0 7225 3761 1

Thorsons

Be inspired to change your life

www.thorsons.com

The latest mind, body and spirit news

Exclusive author interviews

Read extracts from the latest books

Join in mind-expanding discussions

Win great prizes every week

Thorsons catalogue & ordering service

www.thorsons.com

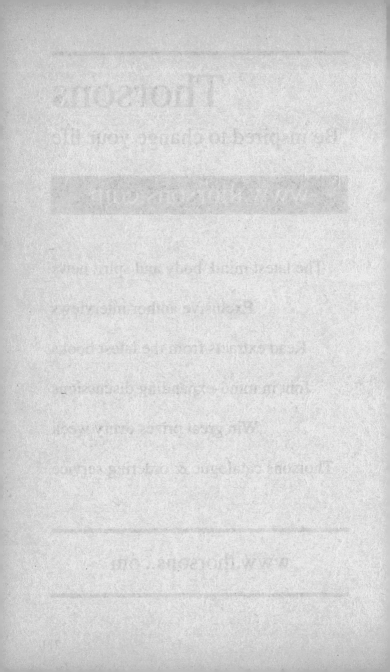

Thorsons

Be inspired to change your life

www.thorsons.com

The latest mind, body and spirit news

Exclusive author interviews

Read extracts from the latest books

Join in mind-expanding discussions

Win great prizes every week

Thorsons catalogue & ordering service

www.thorsons.com